To

M. S. Umar

Best Regards

Aminu

Small and Medium-Sized Enterprises (SMEs) and Poverty Reduction in Africa

Small and Medium-Sized Enterprises (SMEs) and Poverty Reduction in Africa

Strategic Management Perspective

By

Aminu Mamman, Abdul M. Kanu,
Ameen Alharbi and Nabil Baydoun

Cambridge
Scholars
Publishing

Small and Medium-Sized Enterprises (SMEs) and Poverty Reduction
in Africa: Strategic Management Perspective

By Aminu Mamman, Abdul M. Kanu, Ameen Alharbi and Nabil Baydoun

This book first published 2015

Cambridge Scholars Publishing

Lady Stephenson Library, Newcastle upon Tyne, NE6 2PA, UK

British Library Cataloguing in Publication Data
A catalogue record for this book is available from the British Library

ISBN (10): 1-4438-7264-4
ISBN (13): 978-1-4438-7264-5

TABLE OF CONTENTS

Table of Contents

ACKNOWLEDGEMENTS

Our journey and inspiration to write this book started in Africa, where two of the authors were born and bred. We owe a lot to the continent for providing us with the practical experience and opportunity to reflect on the poverty and social challenges facing the continent. Our experiences in the African social and economic environment have provided us with the foundation to study and research the topic of Small and Medium-sized Enterprises (SMEs) as a vehicle for social and economic change, rather than just as an instrument for achieving an individual economic goal. We are grateful to the University of Taibah, Madina, Saudi Arabia for providing one of the authors the opportunity to spend his sabbatical leave at the university to write the significant portion of the book. The tranquil environments of the unique historic city and the university provided significant moments of reflection and focus on the challenges facing policy makers, SME operators and academics wishing to better the conditions of the poor in Africa. We are particularly grateful to the following distinguished academics, leaders and educationists for providing the academic environment to undertake the project: Dr. Adnan Abdullah Suleiman Almazrooa, President of Taibah University, Professor Mahroos Al-Ghabban, Vice President of Taibah University and his consultant Mr. AbuFahad AlSaadi–Director of Self Resource Management.

We are grateful to IDPM, University of Manchester, where three of the authors acquired part of the inspiration to address issues related to poverty in Africa. We are fortunate to be surrounded by colleagues whose main research interests are focused on the establishment of social justice and the eradication of poverty in developing countries. There are a great many people who have provided inspiration, and moral and academic support during the conception and realization of this project. It is not possible to list all of them here. However, mention should be made of academic colleagues at the University of Manchester, especially the members of the Centre for Organizations in Development: Chris Rees, Farhad Hossain, Paul Barry, Beverly Metcalf, Piyawadee Rohitrachoon, Kate Rowland, and David Mundy. We would also like to thank Motolani Agbebi for insightful comments on the draft and Sharmaine Afferion for editing the script. Their contributions have been invaluable to the realization of this project. Finally, we express our sincere gratitude to our dear friend Mohammed

Saghir Umar who introduced one of the authors to personal development literature more than a decade ago. In many ways, significant sections of this book have been influenced by the knowledge gained from the personal development literature and materials.

Aminu Mamman, Abdul M. Kanu, Ameen Alharbi and Nabil Baydoun

CHAPTER ONE

INTRODUCTION

During the last and current centuries the world has experienced significant economic development and a rising standard of living (Blackwood & Lynch, 1994; Cypher & Dietz, 2004; Fishman, 2006; Randall & Theobald, 1998; Stiglitz, 2006). Unfortunately, this development is not evenly spread around the globe. In some developing countries, especially in Africa, the standard of living of many people has declined significantly, leading to poverty and social conflict (Cypher & Dietz, 2004). This has led to the realization that poverty and a falling standard of living, if not addressed, can lead to even more serious social and political conflicts around the world. It is against this backdrop that governments and development agencies have initiated a search for solutions to world poverty, especially in developing countries. Initiatives such as the Poverty Reduction Strategy Papers (PRSPs), International Development Goals (IDGs) and Millennium Development Goals (MDGs) are amongst the most high profile initiatives designed to address world poverty in developing countries (Hulme, 2007; ODI, 2010). Central to these initiatives is the realization that the private sector has a key role to play in the eradication of poverty and the improvement of the standard of living of people (IFAD, 2007; OECD, 2006; Olawale & Garwe, 2010). In a report on pro-poor growth, OECD (2006: 10) pointed out that:

> It is important to recognise that the private sector consists of more than formal businesses. Individuals and households, from rich to poor, also operate as private economic actors when they consume goods and services, sell their labour, farm or produce goods and services. Reducing poverty requires greater efforts to address the needs and maximise the contribution of the many informal enterprises, family-run farms and self-employed men and women that conduct business in developing countries.

In fact, in its 2007 report, IFAD acknowledged the changing role of government and the increasing participation of the private sector in poverty reduction. The report describes radical changes in how the poor make a living in developing countries. For example, in some African countries, governments have largely withdrawn from playing a key role in the organization of economic activities. Instead, the private sector is playing an increasing role even in the delivery of government-funded public services such as health and education. Similarly, in the former centrally-planned economies of Eastern and Central Europe, the role of governments has changed, especially in rural areas. These have ceased to be command economies where the state is a dominant actor in the production and marketing of agricultural outputs. Instead, these activities in the value chain have been taken over by the private sector. The Asian continent has not been left behind in this private sector revolution, but rather has–arguably–been at the forefront of it. For example, IFAD indicated that:

> [I]n Asia, subsistence farmers are increasingly able to produce a marketable surplus, and the barter economy is giving way to a much higher level of monetization. And while state-owned organizations are still active in some developing Asian countries, their contribution to rural economic growth has diminished considerably. Equally, government services are being subjected to new market forces and competition from the private sector. Similarly, in Latin America the economic reforms of the last two decades have led to the opening up of the productive economic activities previously dominated by the state. In fact, it is now recognised that the private sector provides most income-generating activities and job-creation opportunities, and has become the driving force for economic growth and poverty reduction in many developing countries. (IFAD, 2007; Garwe, 2010)

Discussing the importance of the private sector in fighting poverty, a report from the OECD (2006:13) suggests that as a contributor to economic growth and employment creation,

> the private sector has a central place in renewed efforts to reduce poverty and achieve the Millennium Development Goals (MDGs). Developing country governments have a strong interest in fostering a business environment that enables the private sector to flourish and fulfil its role as the main engine of growth.

In fact, the Africa Commission Report sponsored by the former Prime Minister of Great Britain, Tony Blair, acknowledged the need to address the poor productivity of the African private sector as a means of job creation and the eradication of poverty on the continent. The Report suggests that:

Poverty reduction through growth requires a focus on the indigenous private sector, which in sub-Saharan Africa is composed of a myriad of micro, small and medium enterprises, including–the most numerous–the family farm. And it depends on finding ways to help them thrive and grow. Many of these enterprises operate informally. On average, the informal economy in sub-Saharan Africa accounts for 78 per cent of non-agricultural employment, 61 per cent of urban employment and 92 per cent of new jobs. While a daily reality for the majority of people, activities in the informal economy contribute to less than half of GDP. This is because the majority of actors operating in the informal economy are trapped in low productivity activities, where income is low and often irregular. The cost is huge for people's livelihoods, but also for Africa's economies: a productivity cost put at one to two percentage points off growth every year. Marginalised groups and individuals, including migrants, the disabled, and the urban youth, are concentrated in this unregulated part of the economy. (Africa Commission Report, 2005: 231)

1.1 Which Aspects of the Private Sector can Help in the Eradication of Poverty?

Several decades ago, scholars placed the emphasis on the promotion of large-scale enterprises as the major providers of jobs in developing countries. This was apparent in the 19th and 20th centuries when large enterprises were considered to be the engines of economic and technological progress (Klapper, 2002). This approach was adopted by post-colonial governments in Africa through the establishment of gigantic state-owned enterprises as well as the nationalization of foreign ones. Although Small and Medium-Sized Enterprises (SMEs) have also been advocated during the post-colonial era in Africa, when it came to planning to absorb the surplus labour force, much of the emphasis was on developing the agricultural sector and expanding the public sector.

However, the early 1970s witnessed an increased interest in small enterprises as a means of promoting employment in both developed and developing countries (McRobbie, 1981: 103). This interest was manifested by the establishment of SME institutions in a bid to accelerate economic growth and reduce poverty. It is worth noting that in the history of development, the advantages of SMEs have been notably controversial. For example, advocates of SMEs suggested that such enterprises play a very important role in the economy of developing countries by enhancing competition and entrepreneurship (Beck et al., 2004; World Bank, 2004). The competition, they argue, should lead to innovation and the subsequent development of skills and SME success. Beck et al. (2005) further suggested that SMEs are more productive and create more jobs than large enterprises. This view is shared by a number of writers (e.g. Daniels, 1994; Kayanula & Quartey, 2000; Olawale & Garwe, 2010) who indicated that SMEs employ not less than 22 per cent of the adult population in developing countries. We believe this figure is a conservative estimate. For example, Ntsika (2002) reported that in South Africa, Micro Enterprises and SMEs contribute 56 per cent of private sector employment and 36 per cent of the gross domestic product. Also, a few decades ago, Chuta and Liedholm (1985) reported that in Sierra Leone, SMEs employed up to 95 per cent of the country's labour force. In fact, OECD (2006: 28) provided an even stronger argument for the role of the informal sector in economic growth and the eradication of poverty:

> The informal economy forms a large part of the economies of many developing and transition countries. It comprises 42% of value added in Africa, 41% in Latin America and 35% in the transition economies of Europe and the former Soviet Union, compared with 13.5% in OECD countries. The informal economy provides employment and income for many who lose or cannot find work in the formal economy, and it includes a disproportionate number of women, young people and others from disadvantaged groups. For example, it has been estimated that informal employment accounts for 84% of women's employment in sub-Saharan Africa.

Similarly, in developed countries such as the UK where there are more large-scale enterprises, it was reported that SMEs account for 99.8 per cent of all the UK's businesses and provide 56 per cent of non-government jobs. Indeed, Carlsson (1996) and Biggs (2003) argued that SMEs can add dynamism and flexibility to business activities, which will in turn result in improved economic performance. The flexibility of small business structures provides ease-of-entry for persons interested in the SME sector (Amin, 2004) and also benefits those working from home, especially women in highly traditional settings (Floyd and McManus, 2005). Similarly, it has been argued that SMEs are better at using local resources. Thus, resources that would otherwise be wasted will be utilized by small businesses (Amin, 2004; Marsden, 1981; Olawale & Garwe, 2010). This is critical for the development of local economies. An argument has also been advanced that SMEs are able to substitute factors of production and adjust to economic shocks at a faster rate and at a lower cost than larger enterprises (Acs & Audretsch, 1993; Biggs, 2003). Sharing a similar view, Aragón-Sánchez and Sánchez-Marín (2005) stated that SMEs are flexible because of the simplicity of their internal organization which helps them to adopt and respond rapidly to changes. They create dynamism by way of innovating and forming new firms (Beyene, 2002; Biggs, 2003; Olawale & Garwe, 2010). This is a critical issue given the high uncertainty and unpredictability of the business environments of developing countries.

Considerable evidence has been presented over the years to show that small businesses are important in economic stabilization, and that a decline in this sector will have a negative impact on economic growth (Bannock, 1981; Olawale & Garwe, 2010). Luetkenhorst (2004) advanced the view that SMEs are more labour intensive than their larger counterparts in support of the important role of SMEs in the economy. It was also argued that SMEs provide employment and help reduce income inequality. In fact, Gebremariam et al. (2004) examined the impact of SMEs in economic growth and poverty alleviation in the USA. Generally the study found that there is a strong relationship between SMEs, economic growth and poverty reduction. The study further shows that an increase in the percentage share of SMEs' employment had a positive impact on economic growth, thereby reducing poverty. Furthermore, in agriculture-based economies, SMEs provide livelihood opportunities and nurture entrepreneurship. Other advocates of SMEs, such as Todaro and Smith (2003), are of the opinion that SMEs operating in the informal sector can generate surplus income under hostile economic policies such as the denial of access to credit facilities, foreign exchange and tax reduction. Pertaining to SMEs' potential to reduce poverty, Gebremariam et al. (2004) suggested that small businesses contribute to poverty reduction through job creation and economic growth. Robins et al. (2000), also proponents of SMEs, stated that these enterprises have the ability to enrich workers' talents and capabilities. The sector not only provides jobs, but also creates "the prideful sense of being independent" (Pradhan, 1989: 157). These benefits are directly relevant to any effort to eradicate poverty in developing countries, especially in Africa. Experts on African SMEs have also pointed out that SMEs are a significant component of the solution to Africa's development issues (Maas & Herrington, 2006). They maintain that the creation of new, sustainable SMEs is vital to the economic prosperity of Africa, and without them the continent risks economic stagnation (Olawale & Garwe, 2010).

However, in spite of these benefits of SMEs to economic development, there are many opponents who challenge the significance of the role of SMEs in economic development. A number of researchers dispute the argument that SMEs will necessarily play a critical role in economic development and job creation. Their challenge is based on the argument that large-scale enterprises are better at providing stable and quality jobs, higher incomes and more non-wage benefits than SMEs, resulting in a higher standard of living for those they employ (Rosenzweig, 1988; Brown et al., 1990). Other critics, such as Sutton (1997), Caves (1998) and Audretsch and Klepper (2000), share the view that small enterprises have a lower survival capability and their size is negatively related to growth. Audretsch et al. (2000) further stated that small businesses serve as obstacles to economic development by attracting productive and scarce labour from their larger counterparts.

Within these two arguments, there are those who argue that the ultimate goal of SMEs is not to remain small or informal, but rather to graduate into large formal enterprises. In other words, being small and informal is the first step in contributing to poverty reduction. When SMEs formalize, they will at least pay taxes and by so doing contribute to funding the state budget for social support and employment creation. Indeed, formalization can enable SMEs to access state and donor support for the development of the enterprise. Therefore, it can be argued that formalization should be a goal for all SMEs in Africa if they are to ensure a sustainable contribution to poverty reduction. However, this is not to discount the fact that informal SMEs play vital roles in job creation and poverty reduction in Africa. This point will be pursued in the discussions of policy formulation and enterprise management.

1.2 A Further Case for the Role of SMEs in Poverty Reduction

Apart from the inherent benefits of SMEs, there are also other reasons for promoting their development around the world, especially in developed countries. The first reason is the decline of the manufacturing sector in many nations, as reflected in the changing pattern of added value observed in the sector. This has resulted in the dislocation of the labour force from the sector, leading to unemployment and loss of livelihood; especially in those developed countries where the manufacturing sector has been a significant employer. Even within the manufacturing sector, there has been a shift in the economic structure towards service-related manufacturing (UNIDO, 2007). The move towards high-tech-low-labour-intensive manufacturing activities has led to the dislodgement of people from the manufacturing sector.

In fact, UNIDO (2010) has acknowledged the changing pattern of the productive structure of the world economy. The established trend towards service industries observed in the past has been reinforced in recent years. It has been recognized that the service sector has dominated many economies since as early as the 1970s. For example, the service sector represented 58 per cent of world production in 2005. Conversely, the contribution of the agricultural sector fell from 10 per cent in 1970 to 3.6 per cent in 2005. These changes underscore the dominance of the tertiary sector as a key feature of structural change in the global economy. In a nutshell, the world has now reached a stage where economic development, which hitherto relied on the expansion of the manufacturing and agricultural sectors, cannot sustain the growth of the world's population, especially in developing countries. Therefore SMEs, with their bias towards the service sector, have been argued to have a key role in solving unemployment problems generated by structural changes in the world economies (Beyene, 2002; Biggs, 2003; Olawale & Garwe, 2010). The changing pattern of the economy suits the development of SMEs because of the low capital base required to set them up, especially in developing countries. Similarly, there is a high ease-of-entry, which allows the dislodged population from other sectors, such as agriculture and manufacturing, to join the SME sector. The so-called New Public Management in developing countries has led to the massive retrenchment of the workforce in the public sector. This has generated the need to pay attention to the SME sector as a potential solution to unemployment generated by the transformation in the public sector.

The second reason for the growth of the SME sector is the flexibility of SMEs, which enables them to respond to challenges and opportunities in the economy (Amin, 2004; Olawale & Garwe, 2010). This key characteristic has attracted the attention of policy makers and international development agencies in Africa, leading to strong advocacy for the sector leading to the development of SME policies and initiatives (Beaver, 2002; Brinkerhoff, 1999; Dana, 2007; Gibb, 2000; Simon & King, 1999; Manu, 1998). In subsequent chapters of this book, we shall highlight the significance of SMEs in poverty reduction and the role that policy makers, development agencies and SMEs can play to ensure that this objective is achieved.

1.3 The Gap Filled by this Book

In spite of the acknowledgement that SMEs have a significant role to play in poverty eradication, the approach taken by policy makers, development agencies and, dare we say, some experts, leaves much to be desired. In the last few decades, there has been a significant development in SME specific literature which has helped in the understanding of their role in economic and social development. However, we believe that the literature on the issues associated with SMEs' development and their role in poverty reduction is a significant limitation which has led to a compartmentalized approach to SME policy formulation and implementation. This approach has influenced most publications on SMEs, particularly in Africa. There appears, for example, to be a "black box" approach to the acknowledgement of the role of SMEs in Africa's economic development. This approach seems to assume that when SMEs are established, and–in rare cases–technical training is provided, the operators of the enterprises will deliver the expected economic and social benefits. Therefore, advocacy and support for SMEs are undertaken at the macro-level. Where micro issues are addressed, the focus is largely on the technical training of SME operators. Rarely, if at all, are SME policies, SME development, SME roles and SME management treated in a comprehensive and simultaneous way, nor is the personal development of SME operators considered as an element of SME development strategy. The latter is a key omission, given that not all operators have the required qualities to set up and run successful businesses. In an African context where the levels of expertise and institutional support are limited, SME operators, consultants and even policy makers would need to appreciate the interrelationship between these issues; yet SME books and materials deal with these issues in a compartmentalized fashion. The aim of this book is to address this limitation. The book is based on the argument that for SMEs to contribute to sustainable poverty reduction through job creation, we cannot afford to neglect the internal dynamics of enterprise management, policy making or the personal qualities of SME operators. Therefore, the book will address the personal development needs of SME operators. In fact, it has been reported that the failure of SMEs in Sierra Leone to live up to expectations was largely due to poor management practices rather than a lack of finance (Islamic Development Bank, 1994). However, most books and other materials on African SMEs ignore the internal management of SMEs in favour of policy-oriented, financial and technical assistance issues, which are not sufficient to build a total understanding of the challenges and issues associated with the sustainability of SMEs in Africa.

The following reasons have been advanced to explain the slow progress in the development of SMEs in Sierra Leone. Firstly, there is widespread corruption and the total neglect of the sector. Secondly, SMEs in Sierra Leone lack the necessary foreign and advanced technology needed for viable economic growth. Thirdly, SME owner/managers lack the much-needed capital to set up or expand their enterprises (Islamic Development Bank, 1994; Kallon, 1990). Specifically, micro-credit facilities from the banking institutions, NGOs and other agencies are scarce and often discriminate against SME owner/managers. In addition, poor entrepreneurial skills contribute to the slow development of SMEs in the country as a whole (Islamic Development Bank, 1994). Similarly, the absence of an institutional infrastructure for providing training and support to SMEs jeopardizes the sustainability of the SME sector (United Nations, 2000).

The above example clearly underscores the need to address SME challenges simultaneously from the following perspectives: (1) the role of SMEs in economic development and poverty reduction; (2) the development of an enabling business environment and policies that will ensure the accomplishment of SME roles; (3) the effective internal management of SMEs to ensure sustainability and poverty reduction through job creation and decent wages; (4) the personal development of SME operators. Finally, the book underscores the need to contextualize the four perspectives identified above to reflect the African socio-cultural, institutional and economic contexts.

1.4 Aims of the Book

The main aim of this book is to present a thorough discussion of why and how SMEs can help in the fight against poverty in Africa. Specifically, it will examine the barriers that SMEs face in Africa alongside their management practices. The book will further look at the role of SMEs in development. Another aim of the book is to fill the gap in the existing literature by demonstrating, through case studies, the link between SME management and poverty reduction through employment and income generation.

We hope, that after reading the book, the reader will have answers to the following questions: To what extent can the effective management of SMEs contribute to their potential in reducing poverty? How does spiritual poverty contribute to material and general poverty in Africa? What role can spirituality and system thinking play in policy making and SME management within the context of poverty reduction? What are the appropriate poverty-related policies and initiatives that can enable the development of sustainable SMEs in an African context? How can SME purposes and objectives be developed in a poverty reduction context? How can SME business strategy be developed and implemented in a poverty reduction context? What are the personal qualities needed to operate a successful SME in an African context? What is the unique enterprise management approach that is required to deliver poverty reduction objectives in an African context? How do Africa's socio-economic and cultural contexts enable and constrain SMEs' operation?

1.5 Definitions and Classifications

1.5.1 Small and Medium Enterprises

It is widely acknowledged that SMEs are easier to describe than to define (Beaver, 2002; Wickham, 2004). Thus, there is no consensus on the definition of an SME. The majority of definitions or classifications of small businesses are specific to the context within which SMEs are defined or classified (Hallberg, 2000). The definitions vary across countries and regions and according to the size and structure of the economy. For example, the classification of SMEs by the number of employees in countries with large populations, such as China (1.34 billion), India (1.21 billion), the USA (313 million) and Indonesia (237 million), will have a higher cut-off point than countries with smaller populations such as Sierra Leone (6.1 million), Ghana (26 million), Malawi (16 million) and Swaziland (1.2 million). Similarly, the level of economic development can influence the classification of SMEs if the size of capital is used.

In China, SMEs are classified by sector. Manufacturing and construction enterprises with fewer than 2,000 employees, a turnover not exceeding Rmb300 million, or with total assets lower than Rmb400 million, qualify as SMEs. In the retail sector, an enterprise with fewer than 500 employees or a turnover less than Rmb150 million will qualify as an SME. In the wholesale sector, the threshold is 200 employees or a turnover under Rmb300. In the postal/telecommunications and transportation sector, enterprises will qualify as SMEs if their turnover does not exceed Rmb300 million or they have no more than 1,000 (postal) or 3,000 (telecommunications) employees. In the hotel and catering sector, enterprises will qualify as SMEs if they have fewer than 800 employees or a turnover not exceeding Rmb150 million (Hong Kong Trade Development Council, 2012). In comparison to China, with its annual GDP of 9.78 trillion US dollars, smaller African countries such as the Seychelles, Cape Verde, Djibouti, Comoros, and Equatorial Guinea, with populations of less than a million each and a combined annual GDP of 18.8 billion US dollars (IMF, 2011), necessarily classify their SMEs according to their national output and economic activities. Therefore, SMEs are classified according to a number of criteria such as the numbers of employees, the volume of output or sales, and the value of assets employed and energy consumed (ILO, 1998). Nevertheless, the classification and definitions employing the same criteria also differ. For example, in the US, enterprises with fewer than 500 workers are classified as SMEs while in Sierra Leone enterprises with one to twenty employees fall within the definition of SMEs (SLEDIC, 2006). According to Liedholm and Mead (1987), small is a relative phenomenon and definitions change with regard to the use for which they were formulated, and vary within the countries and markets surveyed.

1.6 Some Classifications of SMEs in Africa

With regard to African countries, there are diverse definitions of SMEs, and there is no regional or national consensus on the definition (Sandy, 2003). For example, the Sierra Leone National Industrial Development and Finance Organisation (NIDFO) defines a small enterprise as one owned and managed by Sierra Leoneans, having the potential of employing 1 to 6 workers, and with an investment capital in machinery and equipment not surpassing Le 500,000 (about US$133 equivalent using the 2009 exchange rate). The Sierra Leone Export Development and Investment Company (SLEDIC/SLIEPA) defines the medium as an enterprise owned by Sierra Leoneans with the capability to create employment for 5 to 20 workers, and having a capital investment not exceeding Le 3,000,000 (about US$1000 equivalent using the 2009 exchange rate). The Small and Medium Scale Business Association of Sierra Leone (SMSBASL), in defining small enterprises, uses an employment cut-off point of 1 to 10 employees with a start-up capital of not more than Le 250,000 (about US$75 equivalent using the 2009 exchange rate). In addition, the work of Lidedholm and Chuta (1985) in Sierra Leone defined small enterprises as firms having a maximum of 50 employees.

In Ghana, each major organisation has its own definition of SMEs. For example, the Bank of Ghana, under the Funds for Small and Medium Enterprise Development (FUSMED), defined small and micro enterprises as firms with assets (excluding land) of ¢25 million and ¢5 million in constant 1988 prices (US$100,000 and US$20,000 equivalent) respectively (Osei Boch–Ocansey, 1996: 92). The National Board for Small Scale Industries (NBSSI) considers its working definition for micro and small enterprises as having net assets worth between ¢30 million and ¢300 million (ECU15,000 and ECU120,000) as of June 1996; gross annual sales of between ¢100 million and ¢750 million; and numbers of employees between 10 and 100 persons (NBSSI, 1996).

It is important to point out that classifications of SMEs are subject to change. For example, from a developing country point of view, international development agencies can classify SMEs based on their project objectives. An example of such changes in classification is provided in Box 1-1. It illustrates how the European Union continues to update its classification of SMEs to reflect policy agendas.

Box 1-1. Changes in the Definition of SMEs in the European Union

   The new definition introduces three different categories of enterprise. Each corresponds to a type of relationship which an enterprise might have with another. This distinction is necessary in order to establish a clear picture of an enterprise's economic situation and to exclude those that are not genuine SMEs. In general, most SMEs are autonomous since they are either completely independent or have one or more minority partnerships (each less than 25%) with other enterprises. If that holding rises to no more than 50%, the relationship is deemed to be between partner enterprises. Above that ceiling, the enterprises are linked. Depending on the category in which your enterprise fits, you may have to include data from one or more other enterprises when calculating your own data. The result of the calculation will allow you to check whether you comply with the staff headcount and financial thresholds set by the definition. Enterprises that come above these lose their SME status.
   The first step to qualify as an SME is to be considered as an enterprise. According to the new definition, an enterprise is "any entity engaged in an economic activity, irrespective of its legal form". The wording is not new. It reflects the terminology used by the European Court of Justice in its decisions. By being formally included in the recommendation, the scope of the new SME definition is now clearly marked out. Thus, the self-employed, family firms, partnerships and associations regularly engaged in economic activity may be considered as enterprises. It is the economic activity that is the determining factor, not the legal form.
   Within this category: small enterprises are defined as enterprises which employ fewer than 50 persons and whose annual turnover or annual balance sheet total does not exceed 10 million euro. Micro enterprises are defined as enterprises which employ fewer than 10 persons and whose annual turnover or annual balance sheet total does not exceed 2 million euro.
                    (European Commission, Enterprise and Industry Publication, 2005)

   It is clear from the various definitions of SMEs that there is no single generally accepted definition of an SME (Storey, 1994). Hence, firms defined as small in one country may be defined as medium or large in another country. For example, in many developing countries, firms with over 100 workers are considered large, whereas Europe has an upper limit of 99-499 for medium enterprises (UNIDO, 1996). Some countries like Ghana consider small enterprises as those employing 6 to 9 workers (EMPRETEC Ghana Foundation, 2002) and Vietnam considers enterprises to be small if they have 50-100 workers. Steel and Webster (1990) define small-scale enterprise in Ghana using an employment cut-off point of 30 workers and also classify SMEs into 3 categories: a) micro–employing up to 5 employees; b) very small–employing 6-9 employees; and c) small–having between 10 and 29 employees (ibid.). The diversity of definitions and classifications demands a clear articulation of the characteristics of SMEs and their environment in order to appreciate their role in poverty reduction, the formulation of appropriate policy to support them, and most importantly, to determine how best to develop SMEs and would-be entrepreneurs so that they can perform the poverty reduction role effectively.

The idea of defining SMEs is further complicated when the informal sector is included. Informal enterprises are those consisting of both employed and self-employed workers who practice legal but unregulated activities with cash or barter as the medium of exchange, coupled with inferior working conditions (Edgcomb & Thetford, 2004; Todaro & Smith, 2003). The bulk of SMEs in Africa falls into this category; therefore despite the difficulties, we will include informal SMEs as part of our definition of SMEs because they cannot be ignored given their prominent role in job creation potential. Indeed, to do so is to disregard more than 50 per cent of the private sector (Hernando de Soto, 1989). Therefore, our discussion of policy recommendations and enterprise management will necessarily include implications for SMEs in the informal sector.

1.7 Poverty: Definitions

Poverty is a multidimensional phenomenon, and any attempt to define it without acknowledging its multidimensionality is bound to be counterproductive (Whelan & Whelan, 1995). Similarly, we would argue that any definition of poverty without regard to the context where the "poor" live, is bound to be counterproductive from the point of view of policy formulation and implementation. Therefore poverty, like SMEs, is easier to describe than to define. A wide variety of conceptual and empirical approaches has been used, but not one has gained universal acceptance (see Callan & Nolan, 1991). Poverty is a multidimensional phenomenon related to the inadequacy or lack of social, economic, cultural and political entitlements. This is reflected in the United Nations' definition:

> Fundamentally, poverty is a denial of choices and opportunities, a violation of human dignity. It means lack of basic capacity to participate effectively in society. It means not having enough to feed and clothe a family, not having a school or clinic to go to, not having the land on which to grow

one's food or a job to earn one's living, not having access to credit. It means insecurity, powerlessness and exclusion of individuals, households and communities. It means susceptibility to violence, and it often implies living on marginal or fragile environments, without access to clean water or sanitation. (UN Statement, June 1998–signed by the heads of all UN agencies)

At the World Summit for Social Development, poverty was defined as the:

... lack of income and productive resources sufficient to ensure sustainable livelihoods; hunger and malnutrition; ill health; limited or lack of access to education and other basic services; increased morbidity and mortality from illness; homelessness and inadequate housing; unsafe environments; and social discrimination and exclusion. It is also characterized by a lack of participation in decision-making and in civil, social and cultural life ... poverty in its various forms represents a barrier to communication and access to services, as well as a major health risk, and people living in poverty are particularly vulnerable to the consequences of disasters and conflicts. (United Nations, Department of Economic and Social Affairs: 2005 World Summit for Social Development, Programme of Action)

Some experts have made attempts to operationalize the concept of poverty to enable the identification of those who are poor and what can be done to help them. Probably the most widely applied technique for measuring poverty is the income-based measure (Whelan & Whelan, 1995). For example, the United Nations considers those families living on less than $2 a day to be living below the poverty line. It is worth pointing out that all the dimensions of poverty are interrelated. For instance, income poverty can lead to *health* and *education* poverty; and political poverty (lack of freedom) can lead to economic and education poverty. In most African countries, income poverty is the major challenge for the poor because most of the countries enjoy relative political freedom, albeit with poor governance. Despite such interrelationships and what appears to be a comprehensive perspective on poverty, there is a major omission in the current conceptualization of poverty. One critical element missing in the current conceptualization is *Spiritual Poverty*. The inclusion of the notion of *Spiritual Poverty* in the conceptualization of African poverty is necessary for the following reasons. First, the rampant corruption in many African societies is caused by *spiritual poverty*. There is a *Hausa* word called *Wadatar Zucci*. This basically means contentment with a material and non-material state irrespective of material acquisition. The appropriate translation is *rich consciousness*. In other words, corrupt politicians and public office holders have *poverty consciousness* regardless of their material acquisition–they are *spiritually poor*. Therefore, we cannot tackle income, health and education poverty adequately without tackling *spiritual poverty* amongst those who are in charge of governance and policy implementation. The second reason for the need to include *spiritual poverty* in the conceptualization of African poverty is that policy makers, implementers and SME operators need to be developed to find a deeper meaning to their roles in the wider society, rather than pursuing a professional career and material acquisition to look after themselves, their close families and inner circles. The third reason is that many, if not most economic and social actors such as SME operators and policy makers are not aware, or at best, do not seem to appreciate that they can derive the same pleasure they are seeking from material acquisition, if not more, by developing a *spiritual* approach to their career or livelihood. The final reason for the need to adopt a spiritual approach to the idea of poverty and its eradication in Africa is this: unlike developed countries where there are strong institutions that take the role played by "spirituality", in most African countries, such institutions either do not exist or are ineffective. For example, paying taxes which benefit the tax payer and society as a whole is a "spiritual" act because the tax benefits the tax payer and the wider society. In developed countries people are forced to pay tax whether they like it or not. Similarly, in an Islamic system of governance paying *Zakkat* (similar to tax) is an obligatory act if people earn enough (*nisab*) to warrant payment of *Zakkat*. The proceeds of *Zakkat* are used to look after the *Zakkat* payer and the wider society. This enables the *Zakkat* payer to pursue his/her economic endeavour in an environment devoid of insecurity and social problems. These systems of taxation and *Zakkat* are only possible if there are strong institutions. Therefore, until Africa reaches a stage when institutions become a substitute for individual "spirituality", there is a strong argument for an innovative approach to addressing the gradual destruction of the African social and economic fabric brought about by rampant income and non income poverty.

Within the African context, this book will argue for the expansion of the dimension of poverty to include *spiritual poverty*. By spiritual poverty we mean (broadly speaking) the tendency or proclivity to disregard or to show no or little concern about the impact of one's actions on others. The further elaboration of spirituality and the potential benefits of its characteristics within the business context are presented in the next section and subsequent chapters of the book. The book will be arguing that SME operators who are *spiritually endowed* (rather than *spiritually poor*), irrespective of their religiosity or religion, are more likely to develop a better sense of purpose for their business within the context of poverty reduction. The book will also argue that spiritually endowed SME operators would be more likely to treat their employees and clients better and are therefore more likely to offer a better option for sustainable poverty reduction than the *hardnosed* approach currently advocated by experts of ignoring or neglecting the potential impact of Africa's socio-cultural environment on poverty.

1.8 Spirituality and African Poverty

Spirituality is one of the key concepts introduced in this book to contextualize poverty and SMEs in Africa. We adopt the concept of *spirituality in business* to achieve this aim. *Spirituality in business* has many characteristics similar to the concept of *system thinking* in the sense that it advocates the need for decision makers to realise that their actions impact on others and in return affect them in the long run. The choice of this concept (*spirituality*) is largely because of its value laden perspective which is in tune with the African mindset. A typical African, irrespective of religious affiliation, is fatalistic with an external locus of control. Therefore, an understanding of how this background enables and constrains behaviours within the discourse of poverty is crucial. Although the recent discourse on spirituality might have its roots in religions (organized or not), the concepts of spirituality in business and organizations are not about religion (Ashar & Lane-Maher, 2004; Konz & Ryan, 1999). We would like to make it very clear from the outset that in this book, we adopt the notion of *spirituality in business* rather than spirituality as a theological or religious construct (Ashar & Lane-Maher, 2004; Butts, 1999; Cavanagh, 1999; Emmons, 2000; Konz & Ryan, 1999; Thompson, 2000). In other words, the book does not see spirituality as synonymous with religion, nor does the book take any stand on the virtues or otherwise of any religion. If a particular religion is used at all it will be within the context of its spiritual qualities that can enhance SME operators' personal development and business success. Thus, the book will focus on the positive characteristics of spirituality and how SME operators in Africa can harness these qualities to develop and run successful enterprises. The book will also underscore the significance of *spiritual poverty* as the cornerstone of understanding poverty and its causes within an African context.

What then is *spirituality*? Cavanagh (1999: 189) reported a very popular definition of spirituality because of its simplicity. Spirituality is described "as the desire to find ultimate purpose in life and to live accordingly". Emmon (2000: 4) maintained that spirituality is the personal expression of ultimate concern. We use the term ultimate concern loosely in this book to emphasize the tendency for a *spiritually endowed* SME operator to see his/her endeavour as a means to make a difference in the wider community or society in return for pleasure and contentment. In fact, Robbins (Robbins & Judge, 2010) argued that workplace spirituality is not about organized religious practices, nor is it about God or theology. Instead, workplace spirituality, they argue, recognizes that people have an inner life that nourishes and is nourished by, meaningful work that takes place in the context of community. We therefore share the argument advanced in the following quotation:

> It may be useful to think of spirituality, in addition to the other meanings it took on, as comprised of a set of specific abilities or capacities. Spirituality may be then conceptualized in adaptive, cognitive–motivational terms, and, as such, may underlie a variety of problem-solving skills relevant to everyday life situations. (Emmon, 2000: 8)

The above quotation is a window to other characteristics of spirituality. For example, it has been argued that spiritually endowed organizations or individuals have a clear sense of purpose, a sense of community, and are benevolent, trustworthy, respectful and open-minded (Robbins & Judge, 2010). Other characteristics of spiritually endowed people and organizations include: the feeling of connectedness with others and the environment; and a sense of duty and compassion. These qualities are not only in tune with broader African values, they are also essential qualities that if harnessed and used by SME operators, can help in the running of a successful and sustainable enterprise, and by so doing contribute to poverty eradication.

Perhaps it is worth asking; why bring in the topic of spirituality in business in a book that deals with SMEs and poverty reduction? We believe that, given the level of poverty in various aspects of African lives, a more radical and innovative approach to tackling the issue needs to be taken. This approach must necessarily take into account the African socio-cultural context. Africa and Africans are highly "spiritual". Irrespective of their religious inclination, most Africans believe that their daily life and their economic condition are controlled by supernatural powers. In other words, their destiny is not in their hands. Therefore, any attempt to address the issue of poverty must necessarily include the contextualization of the African perspective of life and livelihood. Indeed, the African Commission Report (2005) has acknowledged the need to address the issue of poverty and development within the African cultural context as it points out:

> At the first meeting of the Commission one of the African Commissioners warned us all that ideas and actions not premised on the cultures of Africa would not work. Ask the big question 'What is development for?', and you get very different answers in different cultures. Many in the developed world see it as being about places like Africa 'catching up'. Development is often described as about increasing choice for individuals. In Africa, by contrast, you might be told that it is something to do with well-being, happiness and membership of a community. An understanding of the cultures of Africa shows that development means putting a greater emphasis on increasing human dignity within a community. (African Commission Report, 2005: 113)

Perhaps the box below provides a better summary of the context of African spirituality as it relates to poverty. Failure to acknowledge such a context would be a disservice to all initiatives aimed at poverty reduction on the continent.

Religious beliefs, movements and networks cross the line between material and spiritual experience. They affect all aspects of how people live, including the social, economic and political parts of their lives. Indeed, many Africans voluntarily associate themselves with religious networks for purposes that go beyond a strictly religious aspect. Religion provides the means to understand and adjust to conflict and tragedy such as AIDS. It provides a language of hope and aspiration. These networks are also plugging Africa into globalization. Senegal's growing Islamic Mouride Brotherhood has an international network that provides significant remittances to the country. Saudi Arabia and the Persian Gulf countries have become part of an African trading network as well as destinations for African migrant workers. African cultural and political systems are being affected by the growth of Islamic movements sponsored by foreign states, something which is resulting in market, labour and ideological shifts. Among other examples, for some women in northern Nigeria, Shari'a law offers a far easier access to divorce than does traditional or civil law. In the Congo the Catholic Church is the only reasonable coherent nationwide organisation, and it even functions as a post office in the absence of any working national postal service. People can go to a Catholic Church in one part of the Congo and leave messages to be transmitted to others elsewhere in the country. In Ethiopia, a ruling from the Patriarch of the Ethiopian Orthodox Church that farmers could work on days previously thought of as religious festivals on which work was forbidden, reportedly led to increases of more than 20 per cent in agricultural productivity. (African Commission Report, 2005: 120)

In the subsequent chapters we will be advocating that the concept of spirituality should be included in the articulation of policy making and implementation. Also, it should be included in the SMEs' and Entrepreneurial development programmes provided by the state and development agencies. This, we believe, can help the continent to make a significant headway into poverty reduction.

CHAPTER TWO

POVERTY:
THEORETICAL AND EMPIRICAL PERSPECTIVES

2.1 Introduction

The previous chapter presented the context of the current debate on poverty and the case for using SMEs as a means of eradicating poverty. Before returning to the subject of SMEs and how they can contribute to poverty eradication, this chapter focuses on the subject of poverty, its causes, and the approaches and interventions taken to eradicate it. Specifically, the chapter will examine the types of international policies for eradicating poverty. Throughout the discussion of the role of SMEs in eradicating poverty, the chapter will be contextualizing the issues to take into account that sub-Saharan Africa has a unique socio-cultural environment that can impact on the effectiveness of any intervention targeted at eradicating poverty. Therefore, rather than presenting theories and statistics on poverty alone, this chapter will draw on the unique characteristics of the African context that will demand that policy makers, academics, concerned activists and experts should look beyond statistics and understand that there is a greater need than ever for the re-conceptualization of the notion of poverty in Africa. The socio-cultural degradation brought about by unrelenting globalization continues to threaten societies on the continent. The effect of globalization has a direct influence on *Spiritual Poverty* (Ahmad, 2003; Hutanwatr, 1998; Oka, 1998; Satha-Anand, 1998), which in turn influences material poverty at individual, family and societal levels. Therefore, poverty in Africa, especially in urban areas, should be seen from the perspectives of socio-cultural degradation in addition to environmental and material degradation.

2.2 The Need for a Holistic View of Poverty

The idea of poverty has been debated by development economists, politicians, activists and policy makers. In the last two decades, the notion of poverty has received significant attention from researchers across many disciplines, leading to various conceptualizations and reclassifications of the meaning of poverty, its causes and the types of interventions needed to mitigate its impact. It is now widely acknowledged that poverty is a multidimensional problem encompassing political, economical, and environmental factors. Apart from its association with income and consumption, the concept of poverty has been related to the insufficiency of health, nutrition, literacy, social relations, security, and psychological well-being.

UNCTAD (2002) considers poverty as a situation in which major parts of the population live at or below an income that is insufficient to meet their basic needs. This definition gives rise to important questions such as: How can the poor be identified? What is meant by basic needs since basic needs vary across societies? Also, although human desires and aspirations might be universal, individuals and societies arrive at those needs and aspirations at different stages. The effective mitigation of poverty and its causes will necessarily require an understanding of the stages of human developmental needs and aspirations. Therefore, the definition of poverty needs to go beyond material deprivation. According to the Australian Agency for International Development (AusAID), poverty is a level of deprivation at which a person is unable to meet the minimum standards of well-being, with well-being defined as: adequate resources for attaining the basic necessities of food, water, shelter and clothing, access to acceptable levels of health and education, accountability from state institutions and civil society, and freedom from excessive vulnerability to adverse shocks (AusAID, 2001). The perspective adopted in this book regards resources that can help eradicate poverty to encompass both material and non-material resources. It should also encompass both social (e.g. *Social Capital*) and psychological (e.g. personality and *spirituality*) resources. Hence, any intervention that fails to access an individual's non-material resources (social and psychological) will not produce sustainable positive outcomes. The failure of many entrepreneurial training programmes aimed at the poor is clear evidence of the inadequacy of providing technical skills and financial capital as the main approach to addressing unemployment and poverty. Our approach adopted in this book is not only the most likely to provide sustainable outcomes, but will be more efficient in targeting and allocating resources for poverty reduction interventions.

2.3 Statistics on Poverty

Statistics on the types and levels of poverty abound. The scope and degree of poverty in a society depends on many factors. In sub-Saharan Africa, the number of poor people increased from 217.2 million in 1987 to 290.9 million in 1990. One of the most disappointing aspects of the statistics highlighted above, which are more than a decade old, is that the level of poverty has not abated, particularly on the African continent. For example, according to the United Nations (2012), in 2008, 47 per cent of the population of sub-Saharan Africa lived on $1.25 a day or less. Similarly, the United Nations Food and Agriculture Organization gave an estimate of 239 million people in sub-Saharan Africa who were either hungry or undernourished in 2010. The recent Human Development Report of 2012 reported that 80 per cent of the world's population lives where income differentials are widening. The same report also indicates that there are 1.1 billion people in developing countries with inadequate access to water.

2.4 Types of Poverty

Various concepts have been used to explain the types of poverty prevalent in many parts of the world. These concepts are briefly highlighted here. Measures that define poverty as either income or consumption below some absolute level constitute the earliest and broadest classifications of poverty measures (Lok-Dessallien, 1999). Absolute poverty is defined according to an absolute minimum standard, often called the poverty line. Absolute is used here to indicate a fixed and minimum set of basic resources which all individuals are said to require in order to physically sustain life. Attention is mounting on reducing absolute poverty as a result of the urgency associated with starvation, malnutrition and other afflictions (Ibid, 1999). In the absence of civil conflict and natural disasters, most African countries are endowed with the natural resources that can eradicate absolute poverty. The challenge is not an ideological one but a "spiritual" one. This relates to ways of harnessing Africa's spiritual potential to provide leverage to change the behaviours of policy makers and SME operators to appreciate their connectedness with the poor and under-privileged. The second significant perspective on poverty defines poverty in relative terms. The most common approach to a relative poverty standard is to choose some income or consumption cut-off point that can be expressed as a proportion of the median for society as a whole (Ray, 1998). This type of poverty compares the lowest bracket of a population with the upper bracket (Lok-Dessallien, 1999). Generally, people are thought to live in relative poverty if their standard of living is significantly less than the general standard of living in a country.

A new entry in the definitions of types of poverty is subjective poverty. By definition, people are said to be in subjective poverty when they feel that they do not have enough to get along (Hagenaars and De Vos, 1988). This definition is based on surveys that use households' own assessments of the minimum or just sufficient amounts of income or consumption needed by the people (Ruggles, 1990). Therefore, if the actual income level is below the amount that people consider to be just sufficient, they are considered to be poor (Hagenaars and De Vos, 1988). A decade ago, IFAD (2001) reported that rural poverty accounts for nearly 63 per cent of poverty worldwide, reaching 90 per cent in China and Bangladesh and between 65 and 90 per cent in sub-Saharan Africa. However, exceptions to this pattern are seen in several Latin American countries, in which poverty is concentrated in urban areas. In its 2011 report, IFAD (2010: 16) reported:

> At least 70 per cent of the world's very poor people are rural, and a large proportion of the poor and hungry are children and young people. Neither of these facts is likely to change in the immediate future, despite widespread urbanization and demographic changes in all regions. South Asia, with the greatest number of poor rural people, and sub-Saharan Africa, with the highest incidence of rural poverty, are the regions worst affected by poverty and hunger.

Another aspect of poverty that has attracted the attention of policy makers and researchers is chronic poverty. This is a concept used to describe persons who are in a state of poverty most of the time. In other words, poverty cohabits almost permanently with the affected persons. It has been argued that chronically poor people are less likely to benefit from national and international developments (Hulme, 2003). Kanu (2004) suggested that people in persistent poverty have known poverty since birth. Their family legacy is one of poverty, illiteracy, and social exclusion. In such cases, poverty is not only about living on less than a certain sum of money per day. Chronic poverty is much deeper and touches all aspects of life. People living in chronic poverty have no choices in many aspects of their lives. To them, chronic poverty means a lack of freedom, the lack of the means to assume one's responsibilities, and enduring the resulting contempt. This type of poverty is characterized by insecurities, which in turn serve to deteriorate people's living conditions.

2.5 So Who is Poor and Where do they Live?

The progress towards poverty eradication will be stunted if there is no proper understanding of the poor. For example, there is a need to understand who they are, where they are located and why they are poor. While poverty is not limited to any ethnic group in the world, research has found a higher concentration of poverty amongst the minority ethnic groups and indigenous populations (Todaro and Smith, 2003). Poverty is more severe for more than 300 million indigenous people in 70 countries. In the developed economies, the poor are mainly amongst single-parent households. Similarly, in developing countries, especially sub-Saharan Africa and Latin America, female headed households make up the majority of the poor (WDR, 1990). For example, in South Africa, a household headed by a resident male has a 28 per cent probability of being poor, whereas a household with a de facto female head has a 48 per cent chance of being poor (Woolard, 2002). In general, women form the majority of the world's poor (Todaro & Smith, 2003). Other poor groups are those coming from poor communities, people living in female headed households with no male bread winners (Ibid, 2003), adults without education, children working under the age of 14 (Todaro & Smith, 2003; WDR, 1990), households with the lowest per capita income, those having many children or economically dependent members, and rural migrants seeking better paid jobs (WDR, 1990). The poor are located in 65 lower income countries. Of these, more than 300 million are believed to live in sub-Saharan Africa (Burnell, 1997). Hulme (2003: 400) reported that sub-Saharan Africa has the highest levels of chronic poverty, while the majority of the world's chronically poor live in South Asia. Similarly, Burnell (1997) reported that 150 million poor people live in East Asia and 100 million in both North Africa/Middle East and Latin America. Sharing this view, WDR (1999) and IFAD (2001) maintained that, "the majority of the poor are found in rural areas, in regions where arable land is scarce, agricultural productivity is low and droughts, floods and environmental degradations are common" (Ibid: 30). This is evident in Latin America where the worst poverty stricken people can be found in arid zones (IFAD, 2001).

2.6 Why are they Poor?

The next section presents the conventional explanations of why people are poor. In this section, we ask the reader to reflect on the question of **why** some individuals, families and, societies are **rich** while others are **poor**. The quotation below is from the Africa Commission Report. It clearly takes a conventional approach to the explanation of the causes of poverty which we believe is inadequate within the African context. This is because there is a danger of passing the responsibility entirely on to the external factors where even those who can afford to make a difference would lose hope in helping to eradicate poverty.

> What makes people poor? The first and most important answer for Africa must be the absence of economic growth in recent decades. For most poor people in Africa, poverty is something they are born into, with little opportunity to escape. Where the large majority of the population is poor and the economy is stagnant, individual characteristics of poor people are less important than the overall context in determining the overall incidence of poverty. And as Africa's economies stagnated while the population grew rapidly, the percentage of people living in poverty grew. This trend persisted into the 1990s, despite the stirrings of economic improvement towards the end of the decade. (Africa Commission Report, 2005: 95)

To argue that the external environment is more important in creating poverty is to exonerate the individual's responsibility for creating the external environment in the first place. *It is the aggregate actions of individuals in Africa that largely created the African Economic Environment.* Some of those responsible for such actions are finding themselves in poverty as we speak. As we argued earlier and continue to argue later, the responsibility for eradicating poverty lies with the poor, the rich and the state and society as a whole. Therefore, we argue for the re-conceptualization of the meaning of poverty to include the notion of *Spiritual Poverty.*

Experts who continue to focus narrowly on studying the poor and the causes of their predicament are unlikely to find sustainable solutions to poverty on the African continent and indeed anywhere. This is because, as the saying goes, *a nation cannot learn how to manufacture its own aircraft by studying a disused grounded aircraft.* Researchers and policy makers should start looking at those who, despite the harsh African socio-economic environment, are able to pull themselves out of poverty. Exclusively focusing on the poor will not help to find a sustainable solution to poverty. This is because any intervention to eradicate or mitigate poverty will require a "fit" between the target of the intervention and the type of intervention. Each poor person, family or society has unique characteristics that led to the poverty. Some causes are self-inflicted (e.g. lacking the adequate essential *motivation* and *spirituality* needed for survival in a hostile environment). Hence, we advocate the study of successful Africans in Africa rather than focusing exclusively on the poor Africans. We need to learn why, despite the harsh socio-economic environment on the continent, some men and women are successful and are pulling others out of poverty. Having highlighted the current limitation to the explanation of why some people are poor, the next section presents the conventional explanations that are widely reported in the literature. Unfortunately, they form the mainstream approach to state and international donor intervention in sub-Saharan Africa.

2.7 Causes of Poverty

The World Development Report (WDR) (2000/2001: 34) maintained that poverty is caused by a number of factors such as a lack of income and assets (basic skills, land, physical assets, and social assets such as networks of contacts) to attain necessities such as food, shelter, clothing, health and education. Another cause is the sense of voicelessness and powerlessness. Also, the WDR identified a vulnerability to adverse shocks as a significant cause of poverty. Indeed, there are several causes of poverty which vary from one society to another. In general, the following are some of the widely reported and documented causes of poverty.

2.7.1 Gender Discrimination

Women in Africa are more likely to be poorer than their male counterparts. According to White and Killick (2001), unskilled women employees earn lower wages than unskilled men who are physically fit to do laborious jobs. At the same time, unskilled women face higher transaction costs in credit due to their lower status in society (Berry, 1993). This reduces the earning capabilities of women and especially households headed by females. This directly leads to women being more prone to poverty compared to their male counterparts. The above statements have to be tempered with some of the realities on the African continent. The changing structure of the economies of Africa coupled with the increasing globalization of the African economies and systems, have led to the mass displacement and unemployment of men. This ensures that women are more likely to be the bread winners in many families. This is a radical departure from the African socio-cultural requirements and expectations. However, given that women are more likely to be employed in lower paid jobs, there is a higher likelihood of poverty in families where women are the bread winners (WDR 2012). It should be pointed out that the issue of poverty and gender would be insignificant if the African tradition of "you are your brother's/sister's keeper" had been practiced as it was in the past. What we have in Africa, as in many parts of the world, is a high divorce rate, leaving women to fend for themselves and their children. So the issue of gender related poverty should be analysed from the socio-cultural degradation of African societies, as well as from economic perspectives. This is where our concept of spiritual poverty comes in. Spiritually endowed people are supposed to be compassionate and benevolent. What appears to be the gradual replacement of such qualities in the pursuit of the material world can be attributed to an overall social degradation in which women and their children are caught up after marriage break-ups. Hence, state intervention in gender-related poverty would necessarily need to address this serious phenomenon. Of course, religious and traditional leaders have a crucial role to play as well. One of the main limitations of capacity building initiatives for women in poverty in Africa is the failure to design an intervention that includes men. Furthermore, there is a significant limitation due to the absence of soft-skills and knowledge that deals with reasons why women and families find themselves in poverty situations in the first place. These are issues we will highlight later in the book.

2.7.2 Environmental Degradation

Land is the main source for the livelihoods of most Africans. Experts point to environmental degradation, such as deforestation, desert encroachment, and soil erosion, as one of the main causes of poverty on the continent. Hence, there is now a significant awareness and concern about environmental degradation around the world. Similarly, there is a significant appreciation that environmental degradation is disproportionately felt by the poor. The World Bank (2001) stated that severe environmental degradation causes a yearly loss of 5-12 million hectares of land, and land degradation affects 65 per cent of African croplands and 40 per cent of croplands in Asia. In the majority of the developing world, the poor often rely on natural resources to meet their basic needs through agricultural production and gathering resources essential for household maintenance, such as water, firewood, and wild plants for consumption and medicine. Hence, the exhaustion and pollution of water sources directly endanger the livelihoods of those who rely on them (Ravenborg, 2003).

2.7.3 Rapid Population Growth

For some people, the reason for poverty is simply because there are too many people chasing too few resources. So population growth within a family or within a nation where resources are scarce will lead to poverty. Of course, this argument is not as simple as that. This is because the issue of distribution has to be put into the equation as well. And when it comes to the issue of distribution, the concept of spiritual poverty will play a significant role in determining whether people buy the idea of redistribution. Turning back to population growth, 6.1 billion people are thought to be living in the world at the beginning of the 21st century, and this is projected to exceed 9.1 billion by 2050 before reaching the peak of 11 billion (Todaro and Smith, 2003). Experience in developing countries, especially Africa, has shown that the larger the family composition, the more difficult it becomes to get food and other basic necessities for the family, especially in a family where the bread winner is unemployed. Todaro and Smith (2003) argued that poor families in developing countries often perceive their children as an economic investment which can be used to supplement farm labour and provide financial help in old age. This rapid growth in population has been argued to lower the income necessary for investment, therefore reducing economic growth, a principal approach to reducing poverty. This, as a result, undermines the prospects for poverty reduction. Schelzig (2005) maintained that the negative effect of rapid population growth is felt more by the poor people who are landless, who will be the first to suffer from cuts in government health and education programs. They will also be the first to bear the impact of environmental damage, as well as the first victims of job cuts due to poor economic growth. Schelzig (2005) also maintained that as rapid population growth surpasses the economy's ability to absorb new entrants to the labour market, unemployment and underemployment will result. In fact, the WDR (2012) reported that each year, 10 million sub-Saharan young people join the labour market. To sum up, large families sustain poverty and increase the severity of inequality (Todaro and Smith, 2003). The factor calls for the adoption of a policy that enables SMEs to absorb the growing number of people who are out of work. However, there is also evidence that families with fewer children or no children are not better off in Africa because the definition of family in Africa goes beyond the nucleus family.

2.7.4 Joblessness

It is undoubtedly true, that in any economy jobs are the main source of income. This means that those who have no jobs are more likely to find themselves in poverty than those who have. The World Development Report (WDR, 2013) indicated that jobs are the main determinant of the living standards of people. The report also indicated that for the vast majority of people around the world, work is the main source of income in the poorest countries of the world. The WDR (2013) also reported that jobs-related events are the most frequent factors that lead to the escape from or the fall into poverty. The main challenge in addressing poverty, especially youth poverty in Africa, lies in changing the mindset of the population to assume some of the responsibilities for creating the jobs rather than relying on their governments to create the jobs. The World Bank study has found that self-initiatives play an important role in boosting income and reducing household poverty.

> Opportunities for gainful work, including in farming and self-employment, offer households the means to increase consumption and reduce its variability. Higher crop yields, access to small off-farm enterprise activities, the migration of family members to cities, and transitions to wage employment are milestones on the path to prosperity. In addition to their fundamental and immediate contribution to earnings, jobs affect other dimensions of well-being, positively and negatively. (WDR, 2013: 76)

Not having a job undermines mental health, especially in countries where wage employment is the norm and the lack of employment opportunities translates into open unemployment rather than underemployment. But a job prone to occupational accidents or work-related diseases can damage physical health or worse. More generally, monetary, non-monetary, and even subjective characteristics of jobs can all have an impact on well-being. Continuing our discussion on the significance of *spiritual poverty* in understanding poverty on the African continent, we have an ally in a person no less than the Harvard-based professor of sociology, Orlando Patterson. In an article titled *Poverty of the Mind*, Patterson (2006) argues that the failure of some people to take up job opportunities is largely due to an ingrained mindset that developed earlier within a community and which discourages such people to take the opportunity to live an independent life rather than a dependent life. As an African American, Patterson (2006: 1) wrote:

Several recent studies have garnered wide attention for reconfirming the tragic disconnection of millions of black youths from the American mainstream. But they also highlighted another crisis: the failure of social scientists to adequately explain the problem, and their inability to come up with any effective strategy to deal with it. The main cause for this shortcoming is a deep-seated dogma that has prevailed in social science and policy circles since the mid-1960s: the rejection of any explanation that invokes a group's cultural attributes—its distinctive attitudes, values and predispositions, and the resulting behaviour of its members—and the relentless preference for relying on structural factors like low incomes, joblessness, poor schools and bad housing.

Patterson (2006: 2) further pointed out that:

What has happened, I think, is that the economic boom years of the 90s and one of the most successful policy initiatives in memory—welfare reform—have made it impossible to ignore the effects of culture. The Clinton administration achieved exactly what policy analysts had long said would pull black men out of their torpor: the economy grew at a rapid pace, providing millions of new jobs at all levels. Yet the jobless black youths simply did not turn up to take them. Instead, the opportunity was seized in large part by immigrants—including many blacks—mainly from Latin America and the Caribbean.

The above assertion indicates that although a job is a major source of escaping poverty, some people might not take the opportunity. We would argue that *spiritual poverty,* which relates to the absence of *a sense of purpose* can result in a state of hopelessness leading to a failure to take the initiative which is required to pursue meaningful means of livelihood such as taking up job opportunities or being self-employed. In other words, people who are *spiritually endowed* will have a clear sense of purpose and will pursue desirable means to live their dreams rather than depend on inadequate and unpredictable handouts. Generating income from work rather than the type of job one does is key to eradicating poverty in Africa. Unfortunately, graduates on the continent seem to focus more on the types of job rather than the income generation aspect of the job. The WDR (2013) reported that simply having work is not what matters in escaping poverty but rather, deriving greater earnings from work will be the key to avoiding poverty through work. The report also found that higher agricultural productivity, the growing commercialization of agriculture, and an increase in cash crop production contributed substantially to poverty reduction.

2.8 International and National Policies and Strategies for Eradicating Poverty

The debate on poverty reduction started in 1973 and was preceded by the speech to the World Bank Governors by the then World Bank President (Mr. McNamara) in Nairobi, Kenya. After the speech the Bank and leading bilateral OECD/DAC members began to re-orient aid policies especially towards poor countries (Riddell, 1987). In spite of the passage of time however, poverty continues to be a significant challenge for many developing countries especially in sub-Saharan Africa. Furthermore, the progress in reducing poverty has not been equal across and within countries. The translation of poverty reduction strategies into effective policies for eradicating poverty with scarce resources has been a challenging task for many countries. We argue in this book that the major mistake committed much earlier by the international donors and nation states in Africa is the neglect of the private sector, especially the SMEs, when formulating policy on poverty reduction. This section examines the policies and strategies for eradicating poverty.

2.8.1 The Growth Approach

During the 1950s and 1960s, there had been a belief amongst experts that growth is the principal means of reducing poverty and improving quality of life (WDR, 1990). The idea of poverty reduction by market-led economic growth was introduced by Adam Smith in the 1770s (Sarwar, 2002). The Smithian idea took prominence until its debunking in the 1930s as a result of the Great Depression. The Smithian idea is based on the argument that the richer a country, the lower its poverty levels and the higher its improvement in education and Human Capital (WDR, 2001). Hence, economic growth is viewed as a powerful force for poverty reduction (Ibid: 45). Therefore, the challenge for countries is how to accelerate growth. However, what is even more challenging, especially in developing countries, is how to redistribute the proceeds of economic growth to benefit the intended target (the poor). We argue in this book that the ability and willingness to redistribute the proceeds of economic growth are functions of the *spiritual endowment* of policy makers and implementers. This argument will be pursued in chapter four.

2.8.2 Good Governance

According to the African Commission Report (2005), growth contributes more rapidly to poverty reduction if the poor are capable of participating in society and the economy. However, the growth literature indicates that growth reduces poverty, but the ability of growth to reduce poverty depends on favourable policies such as macroeconomic stability (Collier and Dollar, 2001; Fischer, 1993), a good governance system (Knack and Keefer, 1995 in Collier and Dollar, 2001) and pro-poor and pro-development trade policies (Collier and Dollar, 2001; Frankel and Romer, 1999). While a good governance system is widely acknowledged as key to good economic management and to reducing poverty, this argument failed to acknowledge the key role of the governors of the economy. Developing a good governance regime in an African context should not ignore the quality of the governors. So far, all interventions on developing a good governance regime in Africa have focused almost exclusively on establishing institutions and systems and providing technical training for the governors. Yet to achieve a sustainable good governance system in Africa, it is essential to understand and incorporate Africa's socio-cultural values into any intervention. For example, Africa's cultural values of humane orientation and compassion for the weak (House et al., 2004) should be integral to the technical training manual. Most importantly, participants on any such technical training programme should be reminded or informed of the significance of spiritual values as a key to developing good governors and governance system. Indeed, as people who pride themselves on being religious, the concept of spiritual poverty or spirituality should not be difficult to introduce in any governance system intervention in Africa.

2.8.3 The Structural Adjustment Approach

The Structural Adjustment Policy (SAP) is one of the World Bank's initiatives which was designed to address the economic underdevelopment and poverty of less developed countries in the 1980s. This was another shift in emphasis from growth approaches to the restructuring of the economies of less developed countries. It is argued that the growth approach was not helping people in developing countries to grow out of poverty; the World Bank introduced a new approach called structural adjustment (Killick, 1998). Therefore, the idea of the structural adjustment loan (SAL thereafter) was introduced in 1980 by the then President of the World Bank, Robert McNamara, in a bid to reduce poverty. The main objective of the initiative was to provide loans for developing countries with a condition for structuring the economies (Easterly, 2005). The SAL provides funds to developing countries that are serious in their aim to improve their balance of payments in return for policy reforms. The policy reform packages are composed of decentralization, privatization, price and trade liberalization, and public sector reforms which include cutting the size of the public sector (Soros, 2002).

The World Bank argued that SAPs as poverty instruments will reduce poverty by stating that SALs are expected to benefit the poor (World Bank, 2003). To reduce poverty through SAPs, the World Bank requires the countries seeking SALs to adopt one of the following measures: reallocate public expenditures in favour of the poor, eliminate distortions and regulations that disadvantage the poor and limit their income-generating opportunities, and/or support safety nets that protect the most vulnerable members of the population. According to Riddell (1987: 98) one reason to put into practice adjustment policies ''is to raise the level of efficiency of already domestic resources and to increase the responsiveness of resource allocation to price changes and market forces''. It is widely acknowledged that the SAP and SAL did not live up to their promise. We argue that one of the reasons for the policy failure is related to the implementation. More specifically, despite the potential limitations of the policy, if the formulators and implementers of the policy had adopted the mindset of system thinking and spirituality, the outcome of the policy would have been much better. Therefore, we advance a novel approach for training and reorienting policy makers and implementers in chapter four.

2.8.4 Foreign Aid Approach

The failure of the growth approach ushered in another emphasis on how to eradicate poverty. Although foreign aid has always been a feature of international relations between developed and developing countries even before independence, it was not until the international community began to focus on poverty and malnutrition that foreign aid became an instrument for poverty reduction.

> Foreign aid can be construed as inter-societal transfers of resources that are intended by all relevant parties, especially the provider, to serve first and foremost the recipients' needs, interest or wants. (Burnell, 1997: 3).

The idea of foreign aid was based on Maynard Keynes' statement that development can be triggered by the willingness of a government to finance investments (Erixon, 2005). Hence, foreign aid has been one of the main approaches by rich countries in the post-colonial era to attempts to improve living conditions in developing countries, and reduce poverty and income inequality (Calderon et al., 2006). Using the Keynesian approach, therefore, the main aim of foreign aid is to promote economic growth in poor countries, which should help the poor find a means of livelihood through employment or self-employment as a result of the development of economic activities. Subsequently, a number of global campaigners such as Kofi Annan, the then UN Secretary General, James Wolfensohn (the former head of the World Bank), Sir Bob Geldof and Bono, as well as NGOs such as Oxfam and others; have been campaigning for an increasing foreign aid. In fact, one of the main objectives of the "Make Poverty History" campaign is to help persuade rich countries to increase aid to 0.7 per cent of their Gross Domestic Product. However, it is widely argued that state and society involvement can be an effective way of reducing poverty. Therefore, Multilateral Development Banks (MDBs) and the International Monetary Fund (IMF) have dedicated concessional resources, including debt relief, to support poverty reduction initiatives in poor countries (Global Poverty Report, 2000).

2.8.5 Trade Approach

Trade liberalization is another approach touted as a solution to poverty in developing countries. Evidence has shown that trade liberalization can provide opportunities for new investment and jobs, and at the same time help in the effective use of resources, resulting in higher productivity. Similarly, trade liberalization increases consumers' access to quality foodstuffs at relatively lower prices (Global Poverty Report, 2000), thereby reducing food poverty. Trade is being widely promoted by many mainstream policy makers as crucial for poor countries to trade their way out of poverty. It argues that trade can help developing countries to promote economic growth and generate the resources for reducing poverty (DFID, 2000). Sharing the same view, Oxfam (2002: 3) maintained that:

> Trade along with migration, communication and dissemination of scientific and technical knowledge, has helped to break the dominance of rampant poverty and pervasiveness of nasty, brutish and short lives that characterized the world.

Some commentators argue that the relationship between trade, poverty and human development is only achievable through economic growth, and that trade is a source of economic growth; and trade liberalization is the policy prescription that leads to trade flow (Malhotra, 2004). According to

Guillermo and Olarreaga (2006) and Bird (2004), trade liberalization provides opportunities through price and market effects. They further maintained that empirical studies show a positive relationship between trade reform on employment and the income of the poor. No doubt trade has direct and indirect effects on poverty and poverty reduction. However, the direction of the impact of trade is not universally positive. It is well known that trade directly affects poverty and poverty reduction through the cost of living, jobs and wages and government revenue; and indirectly through the development and utilization of productive capabilities (Gauci and Karingi, 2007). Also, it has been found that trade openness has had a positive but insignificant impact on the income of the poor (Guillermo and Olarreaga, 2006). The argument is that trade promotes growth and growth reduces poverty.

In 1990, the WDR reported on one of the earliest studies on the potential desirable impact of trade on the lives of the poor in the globalization era. These effects were based on the argument that the poor in middle income countries will gain because most of the exports are labour intensive. Secondly, the removal of bilateral quotas and tariffs will help developing countries benefit by $11.3 billion dollars or more than one-third of their total export. Also, trade expansion may increase employment in the country's textile and clothing industries by about 20 to 40 per cent, thereby reducing poverty in those countries. Finally, trade liberalization may have a lasting effect which might bring benefits to low income countries that rely on primary commodities. Nonetheless, these assumptions depend on the adoption of favourable policies by the countries. Bhagwati and Srinivasan (2002) provide another argument in support of the view that trade reduces poverty by pointing out that if a country wants to maintain an export-led development strategy, it must have a framework for macroeconomic stability. Since macroeconomic stability entails low inflation, it is another route through which trade can have a positive effect on the lives of the poor. However, Todaro (2000: 460) pointed out that, though trade can lead to economic development, it would depend on the reality that, "countries differ in their resource endowments, their economic and social institutions, and their capacities for growth and development". In this vein, it is now widely accepted that the impact of trade liberalization on economic development and poverty reduction in developing countries will vary from country to country.

2.8.6 Poverty Reduction Strategy Paper Approach

An important approach in the late 1990s was an initiative of the World Bank and the International Monetary Fund (IMF). This approach was tied to debt reduction, and it was called the Poverty Reduction Strategy Paper (PRSP) later called Poverty Reduction Strategies (PRS). The PRSP came as a result of increasing concerns and attention regarding the need to improve aid effectiveness and poverty reduction. In reacting to the aid concept, the World Bank and the IMF adopted the Poverty Reduction Strategy Paper's approach in a bid to provide development assistance to low income countries (IMF and IDA, 2002). The process requires the preparation of a Poverty Reduction Strategy so as to enable a country to remain worthy for Bank-Fund assistance (Mahmud, 2006). The approach is considered to be essential in reducing poverty in developing countries, especially in sub-Saharan Africa. It stems from the failure of previous approaches and processes to obtain meaningful breakthroughs in the reduction of poverty in developing countries (Booth, 2001). This new approach came into existence post 1999 to reduce poverty.

PRSPs were central to the provision of development assistance targeted at eradicating poverty. Like the SAP discussed earlier, the PRSP also provided conditionality to any support for poverty reduction initiative. The PRSP was therefore a framework for Highly Indebted Poor Countries (HIPC) to guide all conditional development flows. Given that the PRSP came through the initiative of the IMF and the World Bank, the institutions had to develop corresponding developmental support mechanisms. These were called Poverty Reduction and Growth Facility (PRGF) for the IMF and Poverty Reduction Support Credit (PRSC) for the World Bank. These facilities were designed to support PRSP implementation. It has been argued that the PRSP approach was developed based on the past assessments of the failures and limitations of traditional approaches to development assistance (Piron & Evans, 2005). Unlike previous poverty reduction approaches, the PRSP was very much focused (but not exclusively) on African countries as the following statements affirmed:

> Owing, perhaps, to the origins of the debate in the context of HIPC debt relief, the PRSP approach has tended to focus heavily on countries which are: (i) at the poorer end of the spectrum of countries eligible for concessional lending; (ii) at the more aid-dependent end of the same spectrum; and (iii) predominantly African (Piron & Evans, 2005: 3).

The PRSP was based on the principles of result orientation, comprehensiveness and integration, country-driven and ownership, participation and long-term focus. As a critique, a major weakness of the PRSP was the absence of progress indicators for commitments regarding the private sector including SMEs (Eggenberger-Argote, 2005).

2.8.7 Millennium Development Goals' (MDGs) Approach

The latest international approach to poverty reduction began in 2000. It all began in September of that year, when 147 Heads of State and Government, and 189 nations converged at the United Nations to make the Millennium Declaration [A/RES/55/2]. The leaders committed themselves to the eradication of poverty and hunger, and to improving literacy rates, health care and environmental sustainability through a global partnership. Eight key goals pertaining to these issues are pursued in its Declaration, which projected a 15-year plan that included goals, targets and indicators to attain each goal in every country of focus. The Millennium Declaration was to be guided by a strategic plan composed of 8 goals and 16 targets to be achieved by 2015. The eight goals are: halving extreme poverty and hunger; achieving universal primary education; promoting gender equality; reducing the mortality of the under-fives by two-thirds; reducing maternal mortality by three-quarters; reversing the spread of HIV/AIDS, malaria and TB; ensuring environmental sustainability; and developing a global partnership for development, with targets for aid, trade and debt relief. In a nutshell, an MDG is a comprehensive agreement which represents an unprecedented commitment to the reduction of poverty and ill-health, to gender equality, education, access to clean water and environment.

What is the focus of MDGs apart from their 8 key goals? Unlike previous approaches the MDGs focus on achieving considerable, measurable improvements in people's lives by establishing a yardstick for results. This time action is required from the industrial countries which must help in the implementation of the goals. The measurement of the achievements of the goals is based on 48 indicators selected by international experts. The aggregated 48 indicators at global and regional levels are used by the Secretary-General to prepare an annual report on the progress of the achievements towards the implementation of the Declaration. Developing countries are required to develop a master plan for the implementation of the MDGs.

2.9 Conclusion

This chapter has presented the mainstream literature on the notion of poverty and its causes. We beg to differ that, comprehensive as it is, the literature is not sufficient to capture the concept of poverty in Africa. As a result, the approaches taken to eradicate poverty have largely failed largely due to the emphasis on the macro policy approach or the trickle down approach. We argue throughout this book, that poverty should be conceptualized after understanding the poor as well as the rich. External factors are not the only causes of poverty. A macro policy is not enough to eradicate income poverty from a person suffering from spiritual poverty. Therefore, the proceeding chapters will highlight and operationalize the notion of spiritual poverty within the context of SMEs and poverty reduction in Africa.

CHAPTER THREE

THE IMPACT OF SMES ON EMPLOYMENT AND POVERTY REDUCTION

3.1 Introduction

The previous chapters discussed the arguments regarding the causes of poverty particularly in Africa. We also put forward the argument that earlier efforts to eradicate poverty in Africa have paid lip-service to the private sector; particularly the informal and SME sectors. The contributions of the dominant disciplines and researchers on poverty are inadequate as far as the role of the SME sector in poverty reduction is concerned. In this chapter we discuss the role of the private sector in job creation and poverty reduction. We will then follow this with a discussion of the contribution of the SME sector in job creation and the economy. The chapter concludes with a focus on the challenges facing SMEs in Africa and the initiatives to address them taken by the national governments and international development agencies. The chapter will be re-emphasizing the *spiritual* perspectives on policy formulation, implementation and SME operations.

3.2 The Role of the Private Sector and SMEs in Economic Development

After the neglect of the private sector in the development discourse in the most part of the last century, development agencies and institutions are now waking up to the fact that it is only the private sector that has a reasonable chance of achieving economic and social development in Africa. Several development institutions and governments have now developed policies and initiatives focused on how to use the potential of the private sector to address poverty in Africa and the developing world in general (IFAD, 2007; ODI, 2010; OECD, 2006; World Bank, 2009; 2013). For example, the OECD has developed three approaches as the cornerstone to its strategy for promoting the private sector as the engine of eradicating poverty. They are:

> Encouraging entrepreneurship and investment by lowering the risks and costs of doing business, including by removing barriers to formalization. Identifying and unlocking the potential for economic development in sectors and regions where the poor are concentrated. Using market-based approaches as a way to address obstacles to market development–including support for the promotion of competitive markets and the development of financial markets–and avoid the risks of market distortion if providing direct support to firms. (OECD, 2006: 11)

Until the 1970s, most of the existing literature on the role of business on socio-economic development was largely based on large firms neglecting the SME sector (Cooper and Otley, 1998). However, more recently, the contribution of SMEs to employment creation has attracted much interest and debate among policy makers and academic researchers (Storey, 1994; Birch, 1979; Karlsson et al., 1993). Birch's (1979) empirical work on the relationship between firm size and employment creation attracted the attention of policy makers. Miller (1990) identified that employment growth in small firms is faster than in large firms. Rothwell and Zegfeld (1982) pointed out that Dutch SMEs contributed exceptionally to employment stability during the period 1970-75. Karlsson et al. (1993) also identified in studies conducted on the US economy that new firm births and the expansion of small enterprises were the principal sources of job creation and contributed significantly in the country's economic vitality. SMEs have been acknowledged as major sources of employment creation and income generation in many developing countries. A study conducted by Mead and Liedholm (1998) indicated that a quarter of all working age people in developing countries are engaged in SME activities, although its potential varies from sector to sector across developing countries. Even in the developed countries, SMEs play a very significant role in the economy. What seems evident from the available literature is that the smaller SMEs are more likely to generate jobs than bigger ones. In other words, it is easier to set up a small SME than a big one. There is also an indication that smaller SMEs dominate the African SME sector.

With respect to African countries, Mead (1994) found that the number of employees in the SME sector in Botswana, Kenya, Lesotho, Malawi and Zimbabwe is almost twice the level of employment in registered large-scale enterprises and in the public sector. In fact, Hallberg (2000) pointed out that micro enterprises and small-scale enterprises make up the majority of enterprises with the lion's share of employment. For example, in Ecuador, firms with fewer than 50 workers constituted 99 per cent of firms and 55 per cent of employment in the 1980s. This is also true for Bangladesh where enterprises with fewer than 100 workers made up 99 per cent of enterprises and 58 per cent of employment. In fact, international development institutions are now very active in promoting SMEs as engines of economic growth and poverty reduction. For example, in 2003, the World Bank Review on Small Business Activities committed to the development of the SME sector as one of the key aspects of its strategy to advance economic growth, employment and poverty alleviation. It allocated $2.8 billion to this initiative (Ayyagari; Beck & Demirgüç-Kunt, 2003).

Critiques could rightly ask the question: *where is the empirical evidence supporting the argument that SMEs create jobs and contribute to poverty reduction*? There are several examples of empirical evidence supporting this widely-held view. One such example was provided by Davidson and Delmar (2003). It is perhaps worth describing the methodology used by the authors to arrive at the empirical evidence on the employment potential of SMEs in the economy. Davidson and Delmar (2003) set out to measure the contribution of SMEs to employment creation in Sweden. Raw data was collected from statistics in Sweden and combined with data from three different regions. The Central Firm and Establishment Register, The Register of Company Groups and The Register of Foreign-Owned Companies were used. Furthermore, to create a data set, ten annual versions of each register were combined for the purpose of data analysis. In general, the study found that the SME sector created up to 185,264 jobs during the survey period.

In 2005, Beck et al. undertook a cross-country study of the relationship between various social and economic variables and SMEs. Their study revealed a significant variation in economic growth across the sampled countries ranging from -2% in Zambia to 7% in Ireland. The relationship between the SME sector and the business environment was also examined. The findings showed that GDP per capita growth is positively correlated to the size of the SME sector and business environment. Income inequality and poverty alleviation were found not to be related either with the importance of SMEs or the business environment. The findings further revealed that countries with higher education and more advanced financial sectors have SMEs with a higher employment share than those countries with distorted exchange rates. The business environment was also found to be positively associated with education, monetary stability, financial development and the lack of exchange rate distortions. The authors concluded that countries that create conducive environments to promote competition and commercial contracting have a bigger SME sector. The sampled SMEs in the study contribute significantly to economic development in countries with less ethnic fractionalization than those countries with higher ethnic fractionalization.

Beck et al.'s (2005) study also found that SMEs' employment is positively associated with higher rates of GDP per capita growth, and that their relationship is healthy in non-transition and sub-Saharan countries. The importance of SMEs in any economy showed a statistically and economically significant association with GDP. Hence the authors conclude that, "countries with large SME sectors in manufacturing tend to grow faster" (Beck et al., 2005: 218). In examining the relationship between SMEs, inequality and poverty alleviation, Beck et al. used four dimensions, including assessing the impact of SMEs on the growth rate of the income of the poorest quintile, looking at the relationship between SMEs and changes in income distribution, examining the link between the percentage of poor people and the size of the sector, and thoroughly examining the relationship between poverty indexes and the SME's role in the manufacturing sector. The findings revealed that SMEs influence the poorest and the average people in any country in the same proportion. Also, larger SME sectors show greater income inequality. Finally, no apparent significant relationship existed between SMEs and poverty alleviation. This perhaps supports the argument that while informal SMEs can create jobs, they might not necessarily provide a sustained means of livelihood because of the low wages and job insecurity.

3.2.1 The Potential of SMEs from International Perspective

In another study of the impact of SMEs across countries, Ayyagari; Beck & Demirgüç-Kunt (2003) reported that the importance of the SME sector varies greatly across countries. They found that in some countries (i.e. Azerbaijan, Belarus and Ukraine) less than 5% of the formal work force is employed in SMEs, while in others, (i.e. Chile, Greece and Thailand) more than 80% is employed in the SME sector. The contribution of SMEs to countries' GDP is directly related to the employment generated by the sector. For example, Ayyagari et al. (2003) reported that the ratio of the informal economy relative to GDP varies from 9% in Switzerland to 71% in Thailand. Apparently, these two countries have significant differences in the level of employment in the SME sector, with Thailand accounting for more than 80% of employment in the SME sector. This is a further indication of the significant contribution of the sector to a nation's GDP. What do we mean by the informal economy? The ILO World Employment Report of 1998 provides clear explanations of the categories of economic activities that constitute the informal economy:

> The *small or micro-enterprise sub-sector* is considered the economically stronger and more dynamic element. Typically regarded as an extension of the formal sector, it is held that a significant part of it is usually connected with the formal sector through various types of sub-contracting arrangements. A majority of such enterprises, however, have an independent character and cater to markets at the lower end of the economic scale. The *household-based sub-sector*, where most of the activities are carried out by members of the family (largely unpaid female labour). This sub-sector extends to many different markets, activities, seasons and locations. Most households cannot break out of low incomes and poverty but some households catering to strong markets may evolve into more specialised enterprises. The *independent service sector,* comprising domestic helpers, street-vendors, cleaners, street barbers, shoe-shiners and so on, as well as those referred to as casual labour. Female labour is highly represented in many of these occupations. In terms of size, they constitute the bulk of the informal sector. The occupation is often seasonal, changing, though the change is normally within the boundaries of the sub-sector itself. The skills required by these occupations are the lowest in the informal skill hierarchy. (ILO, 1998: 168; Mitra, 2003: 2)

Is the potential contribution of SMEs to employment generation similar across countries? The answer to this question lies in the Ayyagari et al. (2003) study, where they found that the SME sector's contribution to total employment was significant both in low and high income countries. However, the contribution of SMEs to employment is higher in high income countries than in low income countries. This can be argued in at least two ways. First the contribution of the SMEs had led to the high income. The other possible explanation is that higher income countries are better at providing opportunities for SMEs to grow and provide employment. The most likely explanation is that both the scenarios are correct. In fact, the study found that the SME contribution to GDP is higher in high income countries than in low income countries. The researchers concluded that an increase in the SME sector's contribution to employment is accompanied by an increase in contribution to GDP. Although this finding looks promising for Africa given that most are in need of employment and GDP growth, it is not as rosy as it sounds; given that most African countries are in the low income quadrant. This means that the contribution of SMEs might not be the only solution to increasing unemployment and poverty, unless SMEs are properly supported and developed to reflect the standard in high income countries.

It should be noted that in spite of the potential of the SME sector, its contribution to GDP is much lower than in developed and medium-income countries. This begs the question: given the significant number of SMEs in Africa, why is their overall contribution to GDP lower than in other parts of the world? The answer to this lies in the categories of the SMEs in Africa. Most of the SMEs in Africa are informal micro-enterprises whose activities are unrecorded and their existence is largely at a subsistence level especially in the agricultural and retail sectors. The following quotation perhaps typifies the characteristics of the informal sector in Africa:

> They operate with very little capital or none at all, and utilize a low level of technology and skill. These characteristics therefore imbue them with a low level of productivity, which in turn provides very low and irregular income, and highly unstable employment. Informal sector activities also include activities that are carried out without formal approval from the authorities, and escape the administrative machinery responsible for enforcing legislation and similar instruments. (Miller-Stennett, 2003: 1)

Thus, although the informal sector is more likely to generate employment in Africa because of its lower productivity and significant operational challenges, coupled with the incompetence of many of the operators, its comparative contribution to GDP is invariably going to be lower than its counterparts in the developed countries. Thus, the contribution of the SME sector would depend on the nature of the economy. However, due to the sheer number of informal SMEs in Africa, their proportional contribution to GDP is higher than that of formal SMEs which are smaller in number. For example, in the low income economies of Africa where the informal sector dominates, their proportional contribution to GDP is higher than in the higher income African economies where the informal SMEs are smaller in number. The quotation below confirms this argument:

> The (*formal*) SME sector generates only 15.56% of total GDP in the low-income group compared to 39% in the middle-income group and 51.45% in the high-income group countries. The informal sector follows a reverse trend and is the largest contributor to GDP at 47.2% in the low-income group and contributes only 13% in the high-income group. Interestingly, the joint contribution of the informal and SME sectors to GDP remains approximately constant across income groups at around 65-70 percent. As

income increases however, there is a marked shift from the informal to the SME sector. (Ayyagari et al., 2003: 11)

The above evidence is reflected in the employment generation potential of the two types of SMEs (i.e. formal and informal). In other words, where the informal SME sector dominates the economy as in low income countries, the sector is more likely to be the main generator of employment. Conversely, where the formal SMEs dominate the economy as in high income countries, the sector is more likely to be the main generator of employment. For example, in Ghana, SMEs represent about 92% of Ghanaian businesses and contribute over 80% of employment, while in high income South Africa SMEs contribute about 61% of employment (Abor & Quartey, 2010). More recent data is provided by the same authors (Ayyagari et al., 2007) and reflects the overall contribution by the formal SME sector rather than the informal sector. This point is further explained in the following statements:

> In the developing countries of the low and middle-income group, the informal sector generates a significantly higher portion of median employment than the SME sector. For instance, in the low-income countries, while the informal sector generates 29.14% of total employment, the SME sector generates only 17.56%. In stark contrast, at the high-income level, while the informal sector generates only 15.16%, the SME sector generates 57.24% of the total employment of the country. (Ayyagari et al., 2003: 10)

In fact, the Ayyagari et al. (2003: 10) study reported a steady decline in the contribution of the informal sector to GDP, from the low-income countries (47.2%) to the high-income countries (13%). The study also reported that:

> The sector's contribution to *total* employment also shows a general decline from the low-income group (29.41%) to the high-income group (15.16%), though it increases slightly in the middle-income group. (p. 10).

It is worth pointing out that the age of the SMEs has an influence on their potential to create jobs. After creation, in almost all African countries older SMEs contribute to less employment than younger SMEs. Therefore, in the short to medium term, the potential of SMEs to generate employment is very significant. Therefore, policy makers and concerned stakeholders should focus on these categories of SMEs. However, to ensure the sustainability of the potential of the SMEs, effort should be focused on ensuring that SMEs do not "die at a premature age". We believe the "spiritual perspective" advocated in this book can help achieve this objective. This is because the concept of meaning and the sense of purpose advocated by spirituality ensure that SME operators do not only see their business as an end or a means to make money, but as a "calling" to benefit society, and by so doing benefit themselves. Similarly, by adopting the spiritual perspectives, policy makers and politicians should see policies from long-term perspectives not for sectional, personal or electoral gains.

On the whole, what is clear is that in terms of its contribution to GDP and employment, the informal sector's influence declines as the economy becomes richer. Therefore, it can be argued that there is a correlation between the informal economy and poverty. Hence, to get out of poverty, all efforts should be focused on graduating the informal sector to the formal sector. This is irrespective of the former's contribution to GDP and employment. In a nutshell, although the informal sector has a significant role to play even in some developed countries, its dominance in any economy is a reflection of the lack of sophistication of the economy.

3.2.2 The Potency of SMEs in Poverty Reduction

It is now widely agreed that the performance of SMEs is key to the economic and social development of any country. This is particularly pertinent in African countries where any approach to pull its teeming population out of poverty should be welcomed. The preceding discussion provided adequate empirical and theoretical arguments in support of the positive role that SMEs play in improving the general economic and social conditions of many people; and the country as a whole. The positive impact of SMEs has already been acknowledged by policy makers in Africa and around the world. We shall review the policy initiatives of some African Governments towards SMEs later in the chapter. Here we focus on the unique characteristics of SMEs that enable them to make a significant contribution to economic development and poverty reduction. As we have discussed in the previous sections, SMEs are recognised as engines of growth and poverty reduction through their ability to provide employment. SMEs are able to provide this positive impact largely because of their comparative advantage over large-scale enterprises. This is particularly the case on the African continent where the latter are in short supply. One of their comparative advantages is their tendency to adapt to market conditions (Kayanula & Quartey, 2000). One of the frequently ignored features of the African SMEs in both the formal and informal sectors is their resilience and innovative capacity amidst poor and sometimes non-existent infrastructure and socio-economic instability. Unfortunately, such qualities are yet to be acknowledged and harnessed by specific policy initiatives.

Another key feature of SMEs that enables them to be a source of employment for the poor is that they require low capital to set up and tend to be labour intensive (Liedholm & Mead, 1987; Schmitz, 1995) unlike large-scale enterprises that are embracing modern efficient technologies, which can have a negative impact on the number of people employed if not properly managed. Another feature of SMEs that makes them amenable to job creation and poverty reduction in Africa, is that they can operate in rural as well as urban areas where the poor reside. Kayanula and Quartey (2000) also argued that SMEs can promote a more equitable distribution of income than large firms. This is because unlike large-scale enterprises, SMEs are more regionally dispersed and labour-intensive. Another feature highlighted by the experts is that SMEs tend to improve market efficiency and make productive use of scarce resources. Finally, the demand and supply aspects of SMEs' operations also enable them to act both as suppliers and consumers of goods and services in the domestic, and sometimes in the international market (Berry et al., 2002). Hence, given that economic growth is the key to eradicating poverty in Africa, such economic activities by the SMEs can make a significant contribution to poverty reduction.

3.3 Challenges facing SMEs in Africa

In spite of their potential to contribute to poverty reduction in Africa, SMEs face major challenges to meet their potential. Some of the challenges are from the external environment of the SMEs, while others are from the internal environment–or *self-inflicted*–by the SMEs themselves. The following sections provide a more detailed discussion of the main challenges facing SMEs in both the formal and informal sectors.

3.3.1 General Business Environment

One of the challenges facing SMEs in Africa can best be summarized under the topic of business environment. This can be described as the degree of ease or difficulty in doing business. There are many elements of the business environment. They include the regulatory system, infrastructure (both physical and non-physical), economic policy, the availability and accessibility of human and non-capital (financial and social capital), and national and business culture. Although some elements would have more potency in ensuring the potential of SMEs' contribution to economic growth and poverty reduction, no one element by itself is strong enough to neutralize the effects of the rest of the elements. Therefore, it is essential to have a critical mass of effective elements, a *configuration of elements,* if you like; to ensure the survival and prosperity of businesses, especially SMEs' concerns. Unfortunately, most countries in Africa do not have such a critical mass of the effective elements of the business environment. In fact, sub-Saharan Africa is widely known as the region with the most difficult business environment (Fjose, 2010). However, a *Doing Business* (2010) Report indicates that the business environment of Africa is improving. It should be noted that the relevance of a good business environment to economic growth and poverty reduction cannot be overemphasized (Moyo 2009; IMF 2010). This is because it is the business environment that will enable the creation and sustainability of SMEs, which in turn allows them to employ people and provide them with a means of livelihood. It can be argued that one of the most significant roles of the state is not creating jobs, but creating the business environment that allows jobs to be created. Unfortunately, due to either political reasons or incompetency, many governments in Africa seem to believe that it is their role to create jobs for those willing and able to work. This is highly unrealistic. Even the command economies of the socialist governments of the past have discovered this to be a utopian dream. A model that has been proven to be most effective is not the *free market model* that the Brooking Institutions (World Bank and IMF) are advocating, but the *managed economies* of the East Asian countries like Japan, Taiwan, Malaysia and South Korea. The recent global financial crisis that forced many European countries to buy back financial institutions and prop up the property sector is proof that the business environment, particularly the economic policy cannot be left to the free marketers. In its recent policy brief ODI (2010: 2) made the following statements which partly support our argument against the *hands off* approach to economic management.

> Since the financial crisis, more emphasis has been placed on the role of the state in disciplining and managing the market. In developing countries there is a great deal of government intervention in the market, e.g. through industrial policies that often distort and that are damaging to markets. The time is ripe for a new kind of industrial policy. This would not be about picking winners, or providing subsidies or import protection. Instead, it would be about the intelligent and carefully prioritised use of government policy to encourage and facilitate private sector development in promising high growth sectors, and in a market friendly way.

The above statements further confirm that many development experts are wary of the *laissez-faire* approach to economic management. At the same time, African governments who are in favour of a stricter control of the economy without knowing how to go about it or who are guided by political or sectional expediency, are in danger of strangulating their economies leading to even more poverty and misery for its people.

Turning to the topic of the business environment, a number of researchers have reported a strong correlation between the business environment and the number of SMEs in a country; as well as the number of SMEs per inhabitant (Fjose et al., 2010; IFC, 2006). In other words, the more conducive the business environment, the more likely the number of SMEs in a country will be high. The researchers have also reported that there is a strong correlation between the business environment and the number of SMEs per inhabitant. However, in line with our earlier argument, the researchers also alluded to the idea that certain regulatory elements of the business environment are more important to SMEs than others. Although some experts advocate a liberal regulatory policy to allow the operation of SMEs, within the context of poverty reduction in Africa, we advise caution in certain areas, especially regarding employment and wages. This is because unscrupulous entrepreneurs can take advantage of the vulnerable job seekers. This is why in this book, we adopt a different approach to tackling poverty reduction through the SME sector. The notion of *spirituality* in business, coupled with an appropriate guided policy, should ensure that regulation is not seen as a burden by SME operators. However, for this approach to succeed, the notions of *spiritual poverty* and *spirituality in business* must be introduced to and understood by policy makers and SME operators. The *spiritual perspective* would suggest that policy on SMEs should be geared towards benefiting society as whole, rather than a small section of society. Spirituality advocates system thinking where policy makers, and economic and social actors appreciate that any decision they make will impact on others, the effect of which will rebound on them ultimately–a *boomerang scenario*. Thus, a *spiritual perspective* would suggest that when SMEs support the poor through employment, they are supporting their own businesses. In other words, SME operators need to appreciate through practical means that doing good to the poor makes business sense–*there is money in poverty*. Policy makers also need to appreciate that a good policy should be measured by the outcomes to the SMEs, the poor, and society. They should also appreciate that unnecessary red tape will only lead to the impoverishment of the SMEs, the poor, the institution and the people who created the red tape or liberal policy in the first place. If this was to occur, the whole society would be diminished as witnessed by people in the former command economies. This is why the concept of *spirituality* is vital when dealing with poverty in an African context. So what we advocate here is not a stringent or liberal policy, but a policy geared towards the motivation of SME operators to contribute to poverty reduction, and by doing so, achieve their economic goals. Within an African context, such an aim cannot be achieved through the free market and *hands-off* approach to the governance of the SME sector. The success of China and Indonesia in reducing poverty is partly due to a *hands-on* approach to economic development, where SMEs are guided and supported. SMEs need to be convinced that by paying reasonable wages and employing the poor, it is not going against their economic interests. In fact, if it were, the economy would ground to a halt and the rate of poverty would increase. In the following sections and chapters we will provide a practical means through which *spiritual poverty* and *spirituality in business* can be applied in policy making and in the operation of the SMEs, which should lead to a more sustainable approach to poverty reduction through the SME sector.

3.3.2 Access to Financial Capital

One of the main challenges to SMEs in Africa is access to financial capital. This has been an ongoing issue for several decades. As we will argue later, sometimes the issue is more related to other factors than simply the lack of finance. In fact a renowned development expert pointed out fairly recently that:

> As long as African economies were stagnant, this lack of finance for small firms was not that important. Growth was constrained primarily by a lack of investment opportunities so that the lack of finance was not a binding constraint. (Collier, 2009: 3)

At any rate, indeed there is a shortage of financial capital for some SMEs. However, for some SMEs who still need financial support, access to a market can solve most of their financial problems. This complexity of the lack of finance debate is not adequately understood by the SMEs themselves and some policy makers. The following statements from the OECD's *Policy Insight* summarize the financial challenges facing SMEs in Africa.

> Africa's SMEs have little access to finance, which thus hampers their emergence and eventual growth. Their main sources of capital are their

retained earnings and informal savings and loan associations (tontines), which are unpredictable, not very secure and have little scope for risk sharing because of their regional or sectorial focus. Access to formal finance is poor because of the high risk of default among SMEs and due to inadequate financial facilities. (OECD, 2005: 2)

In fact, for some SMEs who think they need financial support, their problem might be a lack of skills and/or motivation to manage the financial capital they already have. We mention motivation here because as we will elaborate later, some SME operators are either not suited to run businesses at all or are facing "cultural" or "personality" challenges that constrain them from managing whatever asset they have. We argue in this book that failure to appreciate some of the subtle challenges posed by the African cultural environment would render ineffective the good intentions underlying any policy.

Turning back to the need for financial capital, experts have argued that an effective financial system is vital for economic growth (Rajan & Gleacher, 2007). While these authors are referring to a formal financial system, we also argue that an informal financial system at community level will also serve the SMEs, given that informal SMEs dominate most African economies. Besides, in the recent past, some formal financial institutions in Africa, and more recently in the developed world, have not achieved the basic requirements for prudency and trust expected of them. If the concept of *spirituality in business* is developed and entrenched in the business environment, there is no reason why an informal financial system cannot be beneficial to SMEs. In fact, as we speak, informal money transfer is a thriving financial system within communities in Africa and beyond. Somalia relies largely on an informal financial system. However, for such a system (i.e. informal system) to be sustainable *spirituality in business* must be established. Another reason why we believe that reliance on a formal financial system alone will be inadequate for African SMEs is provided by the following statements:

Manifestly, a global recession of uncertain magnitude during which the appetite for risk has collapsed is the worst possible moment to expand investment finance for small African firms. Further, Africa's current financial system is ill-equipped to mediate such flows: it is designed to provide large firms with short-term loans. This is not a viable contractual form for high-risk investment financing. From the perspective of banks, if the investment fails they are exposed to the risk of default whereas if it succeeds they have little participation in the returns. From the perspective of firms, to finance a long-term commitment by means of a short-term facility at a time when banks are likely to be curtailing lending is a recipe for bankruptcy. In a high-risk environment what is most needed is long-term equity. (Collier, 2009: 4)

Another reason why African SMEs cannot rely on the formal financial system alone is the reluctance of commercial banks to offer credit and loans to SMEs, particularly in Africa. For example, some statistics indicate that only 25 per cent of small businesses in South Asia consider access to finance as their major constraint, while in sub-Saharan Africa it is close to 48 per cent. Compared to South Asian SMEs who have a 24.3% credit line or loan in the financial institution, in sub-Saharan Africa the figure is 16.2 per cent (Fjose, 2010).

Soledad and Peria (2009) undertook a study of bank financing to SMEs in Africa. In the study they reported that bank financing to the sector is very limited and more short-term than in other non-African developing countries. According to the report, smaller SMEs are more affected by the banks' approach to financing the sector. They also reported that, compared to non-African developing countries as a whole, where 13.1% of bank loans are allocated to SMEs, in Africa only 5.4% are allocated to SMEs. Again, this further supports our earlier argument where we strongly advocated for an informal financial system to support SMEs in the informal sector particularly. The African culture and tradition, if properly harnessed, can ensure a viable informal financial system. Soledad and Peria (2009) study compared loan approvals between SMEs in Africa and SMEs in the non-African developing world. The findings were disappointing. Again, SMEs in developing countries did better (81.4%) than their counterparts in Africa (68.7%). Perhaps the most disturbing revelation in the study is that African SMEs use three-quarters (72%) of the loans from the bank to finance working capital, whereas SMEs from non-African developing countries use about half (47%) of the loans to finance investments. This revelation is disturbing because a failure to invest will ensure that African SMEs will continue to be less innovative and small. This will certainly reduce their poverty reduction potential, since they cannot improve their ability to employ more people without investing in the business.

Finally, one of the major disadvantages faced by the SMEs in Africa is the excessive cost of lending from the banks. The Soledad and Peria (2009) study reported that:

Fees charged on SME loans in Africa–an average of 1.97 per cent of the loan value for small firms and 1.79 per cent for medium-sized firms–are generally almost twice as high as in other developing economies. Interest rates on SME clients are also 5 to 6 percentage points higher on average in

Africa than elsewhere in the developing world. For instance, banks in Africa charge on average close to 15.6 per cent for loans to their best small firm borrowers, whereas interest rates in other developing countries hardly exceed 11 per cent for these clients.

On the whole, access to financial capital has many advantages for SMEs. As Rajan & Gleacher (2007) pointed out, the availability of finance can lead to more business start-ups that are vital for economic growth and poverty reduction. The authors also pointed out that the availability of external finance is critical for going concerns in order to be able to exploit growth and investment opportunities, which should enable them to reach a profitable and sustainable size. One of the major features of many SMEs in Africa is that they are too small to be profitable and are therefore not sustainable. In fact, many are incapable of providing a decent livelihood for their owners or operators. Finally, the availability of financial capital can enable SMEs to acquire more productive assets such as tools and machinery. This should allow informal SMEs to grow and graduate into formal SMEs.

3.3.3 Corruption and Inefficient Systems

Every business needs efficient, transparent and supporting systems in order to thrive. SMEs in particular, due to their limited resources, are in most need of better systems and support. Unfortunately, SMEs in Africa are amongst the worst served by their institutions and systems (Kiggundu, 2002). This has driven many into the informal sector. In fact, some experts have argued that corruption and red tape have forced many SMEs to move to the informal sector where they can avoid taxation and make their businesses profitable. *So they think.* It was reported that a poor business environment acts as a conduit for reallocating economic activities from large, medium and small companies to micro business enterprises. The implication is that the potential state revenue that will enhance the business environment is lost. Also, resources are reallocated from the productive sectors of the economy to the less productive sectors (Aterido et al., 2009). We would argue that if SME operators use the *spiritual* approach in making this decision, they will realise that avoiding tax is not the solution because the lack of government revenue would mean a lack of the necessary infrastructure and other services for the survival and growth of their businesses. Similarly, using the same perspective of spirituality, policy makers and implementers will realise that the failure to use tax revenue for the reason it was collected would mean that SME operators would desert the formal sector leading to a loss of revenue. This vicious circle is exactly what is happening in most developing countries of Africa and elsewhere. Decades of establishing structures and systems to address this critical issue have delivered an insignificant result other than a huge bureaucracy. For example, the more structures established to tackle tax evasion and corruption, the more corrupt the nation states in Africa become. No amount of technical training and wizardry can stem the tide of corruption unless an innovative approach to addressing the issue is used; hence our advocacy for the *spiritual approach.* At its extreme, it would even lead to a loss of jobs amongst policy makers and policy implementers, or at best underemployment. Many experienced and competent civil servants are underemployed, wasting away waiting for their retirement due to corruption and inefficiency in the system. The whole economy will lose out because as we have seen in the previous sections, the informal sector is less productive compared to the formal SMEs and large businesses. According to the United Nations (2006), corruption is seen as one of the principal obstacles affecting the development of SMEs, especially in developing countries including Africa.

3.3.4 Availability of Infrastructure

The key characteristic of any developed economy is infrastructure. Even the societies that might lack a democratic system or suffer from corruption of some sort, when they have a good infrastructure, they also have a level of poverty that is significantly lower than societies that are saddled with an inefficient infrastructure, or the absence of infrastructure. Infrastructure is an empowering tool that unleashes the potential of a society and individuals regardless of the political and economic system. It provides the means for individuals to discover and apply their potential which can lead to a means of livelihood. The infrastructure that enables people to move and communicate is central for socio-economic development and poverty reduction. Even in the preindustrial age, societies that were blessed with a natural infrastructure such as rivers and a desirable topography to move about easily, tended to have higher social and economic development. For example, they tended to develop more sophisticated language and technology of production compared to inhospitable and landlocked societies; living in mountainous areas for example. Therefore, a transportation system and power are the keys to economic and social development which ultimately sets the foundation for business growth and poverty reduction. Yet these two vital infrastructural elements are the most lacking in the sub-Saharan business environment.

True entrepreneurs can cope with insecurity and corruption but cannot cope with the absence of these vital elements of the business environment.

A recent study has found that an absent or inefficient supply of electricity is by far the most important obstacle facing most businesses in sub-Saharan Africa (Fjose, 2010). This is further compounded by the growing demand and rising cost of vital business input. In fact, the cost of electricity in sub-Saharan Africa is almost twice as costly as in Latin America and Eastern and Central Asia (Fjose, 2010). In this century of economic and social sophistication where integration is a necessity for social and economic development and growth, electricity is energy in more ways than one. It is not only the means of transforming input into output, but it is energy that fuels the ambition and growth of individuals, businesses and society as a whole. Investors within and outside the country will be energised if they believe that there is adequate power in the country that will enable them to run their businesses successfully. Potential innovators and inventors will be energized by the availability of power to be creative since innovation and invention have no set time. Entrepreneurs can leverage the potential of electricity to create new businesses in virtually any sector of the economy. Electricity is directly related to the vital dimensions of poverty namely education, health and income. Businesses in these two sectors also need electricity to function. To put it another way, scientists tell us that darkness has no physical characteristics. On the other hand, light has physical characteristics that can be measured in terms of speed, intensity and scope. From the *Spiritual* and practical points of view, this means that darkness both literally and metaphorically is of limited value to the individual and most importantly to a business. A country without adequate electricity will be in the dark in more ways than one. An individual and a business without adequate light will be in the dark in more ways than one. This means that the presence of light should be the concern of everybody in a community because its absence means backwardness at societal and individual levels. A society that is content with the lack of or an inadequate light is a society that is content with backwardness. In fact, researchers have found that low economic growth is usually preceded by frequent electricity outage (Youpes et. al., 2008). The same researchers predicted that annual GDP growth can increase by 1-2 percentage points with a more stable supply of electricity.

3.3.5 The Challenges of Managerial and "Technical" Skills

We said earlier that some of the challenges facing SMEs are self-inflicted, because many owner operators do not appreciate the magnitude of the influence of managerial competency on the success of SMEs. Many, including policy makers, do not appreciate the most important qualities required to run a business successfully. If we may emphasize, having financial capital is not one of these qualities. Neither is having access to government support. The most important quality to start and run a business successfully is *personal quality*. In fact, we can even argue that the possession of managerial knowledge without the willingness to apply it is not a guarantee for success. This means that technical training or entrepreneurial training that focuses narrowly on *how to run a business* would not offer a *sustainable outcome*. However, SME operators who have *personal qualities* need managerial skills to operate a successful business. Unfortunately, many such operators do not have the basic managerial skills to run a successful business. Such entrepreneurs are blessed with ambition and energy, but a limited sense of what makes a business successful. We shall return to the issue of personal qualities in the subsequent chapters.

3.4 Policy Initiatives towards SMEs in Africa

It goes without saying that the potential of SMEs for eradicating poverty in Africa will not just depend on personal qualities. There is a need for deliberate SME-focused policies by the international development community and most importantly by the state and local governments in Africa. The discussion from the preceding section gave a clear, and broader picture of the barriers affecting the growth and development of SMEs in Africa. SMEs in developed and developing economies including Africa are seen as an important driving force for economic development, employment creation, income opportunities, poverty reduction and regional development. It is generally believed that a conducive and enabling policy and a regulatory environment are vital to the development of SMEs. In the recent past, African governments have recognized the importance of SMEs in the economic development of the continent. They regard the development of SMEs as an important component of their development policy. They have identified the promotion and development of SMEs as their principal objectives for the generation of employment and poverty reduction. In this section, the key SME policies of selected African countries are examined. The formulation and implementation of policies should happen simultaneously. A successful policy implementation effort depends on the effectiveness of SME policy, as well as the philosophy guiding formulation and implementation. We believe that the lack of philosophical underpinning of policy formulation and implementation is the main challenge limiting the sustainability of the outcomes. Objectivity in cultural values is important in the process of formulating policies. SME policy formulation and implementation aimed at poverty reduction are devoid of a *spiritual perspective*. To stress this, Sunkel (1972: 220) stated that,

> A nation must use its tradition, cultures, values, institutions and history to create and achieve its own process of development and national realization.

In order for SMEs to fully demonstrate their potential in creating employment and providing the means of livelihood that will reduce poverty, the existence of a conducive environment is essential to stimulate their growth. The promotion of the SME sector in Africa is winning increasing attention as policy makers address the problem of poverty on the continent. To concur, Storey (1994: 7) stated that:

> Politicians in many countries have emphasised, for at least a decade, the importance of small enterprises as a mechanism for job creation, innovation and long-term development of economies.

Nevertheless, such SME development requires favourable government policies. Governments committed to the promotion, growth and development of SMEs must ensure that an enabling and regulatory framework exists. According to the ECA (2001: 15), such a framework includes first and foremost a stable fiscal and monetary policy setting with reasonable interest rates; a system of financial markets that provides incentives to save and mechanisms to channel savings into investments. For instance, a lower tax rate on initial profits allows firms to retain some earnings and to increase investment as appropriate. Secondly, the framework should consist of policies that minimise the cost of business licensing and registering while safeguarding public interests. Thirdly, it should comprise of policies that facilitate business transactions such as infrastructure development. In addition to the preceding framework, selected African countries are making considerable attempts in terms of policy formulation and implementation for the development of the SME sector. These policies are discussed below.

3.4.1 Improving Regulatory Conditions

Cumbersome and bureaucratic rules have been identified as a major hurdle for SMEs in Africa. In Tanzania, with the help of the *Investor Road Map*, the Government was able to introduce appropriate regulations favourable to the growth of SMEs. For instance, much emphasis was put on the appropriateness of existing and proposed legislation and regulations in the fields of taxation, land use, tendering procedures, training requirements, health and occupational conditions and so on; and how they can be made more suitable for SMEs in addition to the simplification and standardisation of documents, including business registration and licensing, loan applications, purchasing, sub-contracting and tender documents, export documentation and other commercial documents, registration of contracts, simplified tax return forms for SMEs and so on. Furthermore, the Tanzanian Government also stressed the need for regulations to strengthen small enterprises in their access to raw materials and other inputs controlled by monopolistic suppliers, alongside steps taken by local authorities to reduce restrictive regulatory conditions, the facilitation of feasible avenues of legal assistance that could help level the legal playing fields for SMEs; with particular attention to women and young entrepreneurs. In addition, modern regulations on quality standards and recommendations were introduced in order to adopt environmentally friendly production and waste management techniques. This is followed by support aimed at improving the court system, with special consideration for the introduction of a small-claims-court system with outlets spread all over the country, even in small towns and villages (Calcopietro, 1999: 32). In Ethiopia, the Government tried to streamline regulatory conditions by providing a user-friendly environment for the simplification and modification of documents which include business registration and licensing, financial and loan applications, purchasing and sub-contracting (tender) documents, export documentation and other commercial documents, the registration of contracts with municipalities, the authentication of contracts at the notary public, and simplified tax declaration forms for small businesses (Federal Democratic Republic of Ethiopia Ministry of Trade and Industry, 1997: 19).

3.4.2 Establishing Effective Taxation and Incentives Systems

Taxation and its application are some of the main challenges facing African SMEs (EAC, 2009). The Tanzanian Government lowered the rate of corporate taxes for SMEs in order to address the issue of taxation affecting SMEs. An alternative to the existing policy is the exemption of a minimum amount of profit from taxation. This was done to encourage reinvestment. It was also believed that more generous depreciation allowances for SMEs and other businesses could have a similar effect to a tax-free profit level. SMEs were also exempted from import duties on manufacturing input and capital equipment. Given the high cost of tax compliance, SMEs were granted higher write-offs for expenses incurred in training, research, technology transfer and export marketing. Similarly, permission was granted to large firms and banks to deduct from corporate taxes their voluntary contributions to developmental and charitable initiatives. This should allow the private sector to contribute to SME support initiatives that today rely entirely on Government or donor funds (Calcopietro, 1999: 33-34). In order to reduce the transaction cost associated with taxation, the Kenyan Government had an initiative to integrate all the taxes paid by businesses including SMEs (EAC, 2009). This computerised tax management system allows the tax authority to take a single view of affordability by the SMEs in Kenya.

In South Africa, several proposals have been made with respect to the differential treatment of small enterprises so that the tax burden can be reduced and reinvestment facilitated. In this view, a number of proposals were highlighted which are summarized as follows: a lower rate of corporate taxes for small enterprises, and the exemption of a minimum amount of profit from taxation, so as to encourage reinvestment; the provision of depreciation allowances, exemptions from or rebates on import duties on manufacturing inputs and capital equipment, writing-off expenses incurred as a result of tax compliance, a tax incentive to stimulate subcontracting by large firms and a greater volume of loans to SMEs; a tax incentive to help overcome the gender bias of larger firms and service establishments vis-à-vis SMEs owned by women, and the promotion of small enterprises through the differentiation of rates and user charges at the local authority and Regional Services Council (RSC) (South Africa Department of Trade and Industry, 1995).

3.4.3 Financial Assistance Policy

We have extensively discussed the issues associated with the lack of availability of financial capital for SMEs. In order to increase SMEs' access to finance in South Africa, the Government promulgated a policy which encourages larger commercial banks to establish divisions that deal specifically with small business financing. In addition, SME-focused financing institutions were established, which consist of institutions originating from the sector and mostly backed by either government, financing or foreign donor money. The policy also includes micro-enterprise finance. These are NGOs with the specific goal of financing the SME sector. Added to this, it comprises of venture finance–equity funds to address the equity needs of SMEs. A credit guarantee scheme was also established to strengthen the commercialized funding of SMEs, based on a differentiated credit guarantee system, alongside deposit-taking by lending NGOs, which enables the mobilization of funds for micro-loans. Finally, an alternative collateral system was put in place in order to more readily increase the accessibility of commercial funds. To help this further, recognition is given to other types of securities and collateral substitutes, especially in rural areas where land for example is still held communally (South Africa Department of Trade and Industry, 1995).

In Tanzania, the National Income Generation Programme (NIGP) works with six private banks on the design, capitalization and implementation of a Mutual Credit Guarantee Scheme to enhance the sale of good quality products to graduate SMEs with insufficient collateral to obtain bank credit. Additionally, other mechanisms were put in place to assist the process of the SMEs' accessibility to credit consisting of guarantee funds created by self-help organizations on the basis of member contributions with the aim to issue credit guarantees only to their members. Also, guarantee funds were created by self-help organizations with donor grants to serve the needs of their clients (Calcopietro, 1999: 34).

3.4.4 Infrastructure policy

The availability and accessibility of good and sustainable infrastructure facilities create a favourable environment for productive activities to take place. In the modern economy, there can be no successful and productive SMEs without electricity, water, good roads, and telecommunication systems, as suggested by (Economic Commission for Africa, 2001: 22):

The importance of this function has increased in recent years, because of the changing nature of competition in regional and global markets. Speedy and punctual delivery of manufactured goods has become a major parameter in the new competition. A well developed infrastructure–for moving goods from factories to ports and for rapid international communication significantly reduces the transaction costs involved in exporting. Bottlenecks in sea and air cargo space and high charges feed into non competitive pricing, missed deadlines, poor reputation and cancellation of orders. Long delays in obtaining telephone and electricity connections raise production costs and waste scarce management time.

The Ethiopian Government improves the infrastructure of SMEs by developing and improving the road network, power, water and telecommunication. Added to this, the private sector was allowed to give a helping hand in the development of certain infrastructure to boost government undertakings. The government effort in building and improving SME infrastructure is also being supported by the regional governments, development associations and NGOs (Federal Democratic Republic of Ethiopia Ministry of Trade and Industry, 1997: 24). The Nigerian Government has embarked on a massive infrastructural development programme that should ultimately boast economic activities in general and the SME sector in particular. In South Africa, parastatals such as Eskon, Transnet/Intersite and the regional development corporations with the help of the government have been charged with the responsibility of improving the supply of electricity to businesses, basic services and road infrastructure in commercial and industrial areas; in addition to improving facilities for fresh produce and other markets, telecommunications, postal delivery services and so on (South Africa Department of Trade and Industry, 1995).

3.4.5 Supporting Access to Technology

The availability and accessibility of appropriate technology are key barriers to SME growth in Africa. The application of information and communication can be a great leveller to SMEs (Hall, 2000). Access to technology can provide a significant competitive advantage to enterprises that have the skills to use it. For instance, SMEs can use information technology to create value and compete with their larger counterparts in a less biased environment (Botswana Ministry of Commerce and Industry, 1999). However, SMEs' limited access to technology reduces their potential for acquiring and maximizing the benefits of technology. Furthermore, technological change can put SMEs at risk if they do not keep up or lead their competitors (Botswana Ministry of Commerce and Industry, 1999). Improving technology in the SME sector is important for the development of the sector and the economies of developed and developing countries.

In Namibia, the Government, under the aegis of the Ministry of Trade and Industry, improved access to technology by introducing a technology sourcing programme in a bid to help establish an international base on technology for small businesses. Likewise, satellite demonstration centres were established in the country (Erastus-Sacharia et al., 1999). Regarding access to technology, the Ethiopian Government increased access to technology by strengthening the relevance and effectiveness of existing Research and Development (R&D) institutions and centres to support SMEs. The government also disseminated R&D outputs to SMEs through extension agents, and finally by establishing a technology database (Federal Democratic Republic of Ethiopia Ministry of Trade and Industry, 1997: 24). There are more recent developments in the area of ICT that are aimed at giving the SME sector access to technology. For example, Kenya is now one of the leading countries in the world (not Africa) regarding mobile banking.

3.4.6 Export Promotion

The formal SME sector can be a major contributor to export growth. For example, SMEs in the South East Asian region have played, and continue to play, a significant role in international trade, which led to a significant drop in unemployment and poverty reduction in the last century. The competitiveness of SMEs in Africa can be strengthened by the removal of the anti-export bias that exists in most African countries (Thoburn, 2000). In 1995 the Ghanaian Government enacted the Free Zones Act (Act 504), alongside the creation of the Ghana Free Zones Board (Aryeetey and Ahene, 2005). The Free Zones Act encourages firms that export more than 70 per cent of their annual production to receive a 10-year tax holiday which is tax free, with an 8% tax credit after the tax holiday. In addition, the government tax non-traditional exporters 8% with exemption from several export duties (Ibid, 2005). In South Africa, the government supports small enterprise export by encouraging the development of export support programmes such as a finance scheme, exhibition facilities, new types of export trading houses, adjusted export credit-guarantee schemes, an expansion of the export marketing assistance scheme, and special training efforts which are designed to meet the needs of the bigger exporters (South Africa Department of Trade and Industry, 1995). In Nigeria, several state initiatives have been enacted to boost exports by the SME sector. For example, the Export Promotion Commission has been established. It works with many SME umbrella organizations and SME support institutions such as the Small and Medium Enterprises Development Agency of Nigeria (SMEDA) and the Manufacturers' Association of Nigeria (MAN) to encourage the export ambitions and goals of SMEs.

3.4.7 Training in Entrepreneurship, Skills and Management

We have already highlighted the issue of the lack of availability of technical and managerial skills in Africa. The lack of skilled labour and poor management are factors affecting the development of SMEs and their potential in achieving employment provision and poverty reduction in developing countries. To improve training in entrepreneurship skills and management within the SME sector in Tanzania, the Government established the Vocational and Educational Training Authority (VETA), which provides vocational education and training to would-be entrepreneurs. The school provided training in areas such as carpentry, masonry, bricklaying and tailoring (Calcopietro, 1999). In Namibia, the state, through the National Vocational Training Fund Act, spent N$80 million under the auspices of the National Training Board to provide grants to training institutions or directly to entrepreneurs in addition to providing soft loans to entrepreneurs. Also, the Ministry of Basic Education and Culture provides adult skills' development, and vocational and entrepreneurship training. The Department of Agriculture and Rural Development provides training for NGOs working alongside co-operatives (Erastus-Sacharia et al., 1999). In Nigeria, the Government established the National Directorate of Employment with the sole aim of solving unemployment through the provision of skills to the unemployed and would-be entrepreneurs. Again, one of the main shortcomings of almost all the training programs is the underlying assumption that all unemployed people will be able to run a successful business if they are provided with technical skills. The other assumption is that even the able would-be entrepreneurs have the motivation to help eradicate poverty through running a successful SME. We believe, unless such assumptions are revisited, it is unlikely that the training programs will deliver a sustainable outcome. We believe the failure of such initiatives to deliver desirable outcomes is largely due to the failure to choose the right people and train them in the right way. While almost every policy maker knows that not all people can be medical doctors or engineers, for inexplicable reasons, he/she appear to assume that every unemployed person can run a business.

3.4.8 Advancing Opportunities for Women and Young People

One way to fight poverty is to empower women and young people. When a woman is financially better off, the entire family will be better off. Women have the ability to make better use of capital with lower investment and produce a higher rate of return on investments (Todaro &

Smith, 2003). It has been argued that the success of the Gremin Bank experiment in Bangladesh is largely due to the choice of the target (i.e. women). It is unlikely that the experiment would deliver the same initial level of success if men had been chosen as the target. A number of SME studies in Africa have shown that the sector is dominated by female entrepreneurs. Therefore, it is vital for African governments to formulate policies that work against discriminatory barriers affecting women in the SME sector. According to Haftendorn (2003), there are nearly 300 million unemployed and underemployed young people between the ages of 16 and 30 years globally. Twenty per cent of these young people are potential entrepreneurs, but less than 5 per cent manage to achieve this. In Namibia, the Ministry of Youth and Sports established youth development programmes alongside skill training centres such as the Youth Promotion Centre in Katutura to improve opportunities for young men to engage in the SME sector. Also, the Department of Women's Affairs empowers women's participation in the SME sector by providing advisory services and financial support for income generating activities (Erastus-Sacharia et al., 1999). With regard to advancing opportunities for women and young people, the Ethiopian Government formulated a National Policy on Ethiopian Women with the objective of eliminating gender and cultural bias that prevents women from participating in the country's main economic stream and guarantees gender equality. The Department of Women's Affairs was created to help in the implementation of policies for women's affairs and to determine whether policies, programmes and development plans published by the government are favourable to women (Stevenson and St-Onge, 2005).

3.4.9 Supporting Agencies

In the last couple of decades, having realised the potential of SMEs in economic development, several African governments have established agencies with the sole mandate of supporting SMEs. Some of these agencies include financial agencies such as commercial banks and non-financial agencies such as regulatory and supporting institutions. Such agencies collaborate with independent SME umbrella organizations and international development agencies such as UNIDO, UNDP, ILO, etc., to support local SMEs. For example, over the years Nigeria has established financial and non-financial agencies to support the SME sector. Some of these agencies include the Nigerian Bank of Industry; the Nigerian Export-Import Bank; the National Directorate of Employment; the People's Bank of Nigeria; the Community Bank; the National Poverty Eradication

Programme (NAPEP); the Bank of Industry; the Nigerian Agric Cooperation and Rural Development Bank; and the Small and Medium Enterprises Development Agency of Nigeria (SMEDAN). SMEDAN in particular plays the following roles shown in Box 3-1 below.

Box 3-1. Roles of SMEDAN in Nigeria

Source, process and disseminate business information
• Create and regularly update a data bank on MSMEs, raw materials, markets, available local technologies/machinery and prototypes.

Policy development
• Formulate and ensure due approval and implementation of an MSME policy for Nigeria;
• Conduct impact assessment studies and use the same to recommend improvements in policy intervention;
• Conduct regular stakeholders' for a.

Establish Business Support Centres (BSCs) to provide the following services:
• Model business planning skills;
• Mentor professional service such as accounting, financing and book keeping;
• Industrial dynamics and technology assessment;
• Legal and taxation advisory services;
• Demonstration models to provide sector service providers.

General business consultation
• Capacity building and promotional services;
• Vertical linkages of MSMEs with large enterprises;
• Organization of MSMEs into clusters and co-operatives to enhance their productivity and have easier access to factors of production, including finance;
• Arrangement/facilitation of trade and technological exposition;
• Provision of a market support information system through the Agency's website;
• Encouragement and facilitation of new investments in designated priority areas in each State of the federation;
• Establishment of industrial parks;
• SMEDAN, through a public private sector partnership, is facilitating the establishment of industrial parks and regional SME development centres;
• Each park comes with industrial buildings, and offers MSMEs the following facilities on a cost-sharing basis;
• Security, electricity, water, buying centres, service providers, petrol stations and capital intensive technologies.

Enhance MSMEs' access to finance
- Liaise with financial institutions to harness and pool resources for utilization by MSMEs;
- Attract foreign investment and funds for the development of the MSME sub-sector;
- Constantly liaise with other institutions for the establishment and operation of an MSME Credit Guarantee Scheme;
- Networking; SMEDAN is partnering with trade Groups, NGOs, Government Ministries and Agencies, research and technological institutions and multilateral/donor agencies, etc.

Source: http://www.smedan.org/core-services.html

3.5 Initiatives by International Development Agencies

Several international development agencies, namely World Bank (2005; 2009), OECD (2006), IFAD (2011), ILO (2012), and UNIDO (2011) have developed programmes and initiatives to help the SME sector and the private sector in general. For example, IFAD (2011) has what is calls a private sector development and partnership initiative. The programme is described as follows:

> The goal of the private-sector development and partnership (PSDP) strategy is to engage the private sector to bring more benefits and resources to IFAD's target group, the rural poor. The more immediate objective of the strategy is to increase pro-poor private-sector operations and investment in rural areas. (IFAD, 2011: 22)

To achieve the objectives of PSDP, IFAD engages policy makers in dialogue with the main aim of providing the enabling policy and institutional environment for the development of the private sector. Another initiative by an international agency is the development of tools and operational instruments by the International Finance Corporation (IFC) of the World Bank. For example, the IFC developed an SME tool kit which helps SME operators with information and techniques for running a successful business. The information and instruments are provided free of charge through an online database at www.smetoolkit.org. The advantage of such a toolkit is that it is customized to reflect the local business environment. A further important initiative by an international development agency is the famous International Labour Office's (ILO) Start and Improve Your Business (SIYB) Program. This program, which started in the 1980s, provides training to trainers and SME operators on how to start and run a successful business enterprise. The program's main purpose is to help reduce youth unemployment in developing countries through the creation of businesses. Box 3-2 provides a summary of a report commissioned by the ILO to evaluate the impact of SIYB across countries.

Box 3-2. Start and Improve Your Business Global Tracer Study

Since its initial conception in the 1980s (IYB) and 1990s (SYB), the SIYB training programme has spread to 100 countries. It has so far reached 17,000 trainers, more than 200 MTs and at least 2,500 training providers from the public and private sectors. It is relevant because it fulfils existing and emerging demands from (potential) entrepreneurs, trainers and organizations. The programme meets their needs with simple, low-cost and comprehensive materials and methods to train people in setting up and running a small business. The introduction of SIYB has helped to improve the personal and institutional competences of many trainers and partners. Trainers have gained valuable insight, enhanced their business-related knowledge and skills and improved their own entrepreneurial attitudes. Over the years, at least 4.5 million people have accessed SYB and IYB training sessions, as reported by SIYB partner organizations. An estimated two out of three trainees were undertaking formal or informal business activities at the time of training. Only one third of SYB trainees were not yet in business, out of which one third were actually able to start up a new business. The SIYB training can provoke significant changes at the entrepreneur level. Positive impacts include new business start-ups, increased product diversification, cost savings and increased profits. This contributes to income generation and jobs in the micro-, small and medium enterprise sector. In a newly-started business, three jobs are created on average, including the business owner's job. In an existing business, on average, one extra job is generated. The SIYB is a materials-based training package, and the SYB and IYB manuals remain the backbone of the programme. So far, SIYB manuals have been translated into 32 languages, and various sector-specific adaptations exist in certain regions. Simplified versions have also been created for certain regions.

Source: *Start and Improve Your Business Global Tracer Study 2011: ILO's Business Management Training Programme. (ILO, 2012: 23-25)*

The report by the ILO tracer survey finally concluded with the following statements:

> Both the results of this outreach study, as well as the latest results of large-scale randomized control trials on impact, underscore the importance and continued relevance of small business management training for job creation. The numbers in this report, and the details collected, show that the outreach of SIYB is likely to increase considerably in the future. The Chinese Government is using the package as its core tool and trainee numbers are increasing rapidly. In 2012, in India, SIYB will be introduced on a larger scale. A range of ILO projects and partner organizations in countries as diverse as Senegal, Indonesia, Guatemala, Kenya, South Africa and Zambia will start to use SIYB in a variety of different contexts, including in vocational training institutions, as a tool for public employment services, or as a business services tool in value chain development projects. (ILO, 2012: 27)

Other support provided by the international development agencies includes financial support. For example, The World Bank Group has devoted $10 billion to support programs aimed at supporting SMEs. However, it should be pointed out that the direction of financial support to SMEs has shifted from subsidizing SMEs to capacity building, especially for policy makers, in order to develop and implement SME-sensitive policies.

3.6 Conclusion

This chapter has highlighted the significant role of the private sector and SMEs in job creation and poverty reduction. However, the chapter has underscored the challenges faced by SMEs in Africa and has called for governments and development agencies to take an innovative approach in providing good policies and support for SME operators. In particular, the chapter argues that, through the use of the concept *spirituality in business,* policy makers can develop poverty-focused initiatives that can benefit SMEs and society at large. Similarly, the chapter argues that if SME operators are sensitised with the benefits of *spirituality in business*, they will operate in a way that will be more sustainable in the long run. The chapter concludes by advocating that training targeted at entrepreneurs should not focus on technical training alone. There is a need to address the personal development dimension of SME operators. This is because there are specific personal qualities required to run a successful business.

CHAPTER FOUR

THE FOUNDATION OF SME POLICY MAKING AND ENTREPRENEURSHIP IN THE FIGHT AGAINST POVERTY IN AFRICA

4.1 Introduction

The role of Small and Medium-sized Enterprises (SMEs) in poverty reduction has gained more traction over the past two decades particularly in developing countries. While much focus has been on SME creation and development, this book argues that for SMEs to contribute to sustainable poverty reduction there is a need to focus on the personal qualities of policy makers and SME operators. With the aid of the concept of spirituality and system thinking, this chapter proposes how African policy makers and SME operators can be reoriented to ensure that their attitudes and behaviour are in tune with poverty reduction rather than rent-seeking behaviour or narrow personal or sectional interests which in the long-term have a negative impact on them in addition to the impact on society. Central to the paper is the argument that previous "neutral" approaches to developing policy makers and SME operators are devoid of the cultural context of Africa. The paper argues that sensitising policy makers, SME operators and prospective entrepreneurs using the concepts and ideas they understand and believe in will have more potency in changing behaviour.

This chapter focuses on the issue of how to develop policy makers, relevant public servants, prospective entrepreneurs and SME operators to enable poverty reduction through job creation. The paper uses the concept of *spirituality* and *system thinking* to demonstrate the importance of developing appropriate behaviours amongst policy makers and business operators that can have mutual benefits across all stakeholders in society. We set out to write a paper that fits with the socio-cultural context of Africa, especially sub-Saharan Africa. At first we thought *system thinking* would provide a foundation to write a culturally sensitive and relevant paper on how the SME sector and prospective entrepreneurs can help with poverty reduction through job creation. However, our search also unearthed the concept of *spirituality* which we believe is more in tune with the African belief system which influences the behaviour of public servants and business operators (Nussbaum, 2003; Van Dyk, 2001). The choice of spirituality as an idea to underpin our discussion of the socio-cultural context of Africa is because "*fatalism*" and an *external locus of control* have been argued to be part of the cultural beliefs in Africa (House et al., 2004; Mbiti, 1991; Mamman, Baydoun & Asumah, 2009). These concepts basically assert that something or someone has a significant influence on a person's state of material and physical being. *Ubuntu,* which is an African philosophy of life and livelihood, is also in tune with the notion of spirituality discussed in this paper. *Ubuntu* advocates unity, common interests and destiny (Mbiti, 1991; Lessem & Nussbaum, 1996; Nussbaum, 2003). This is encapsulated in the African saying: *I am happy if you are* or the Christian doctrine of *love thy neighbour as you love thy self* or the Islamic teaching that *no one is a true believer until he likes for his brother what he likes for himself.* However, we argue that the exclusiveness of the application of organized religious teachings (not the religious scriptures) as well as the philosophy of *Ubuntu* make them less potent in addressing the challenges of poverty and underdevelopment in Africa. Spirituality on the other hand is much more inclusive and can therefore be operationalized across the diversity of ethnicity and religions on the continent. Therefore the paper advocates that interventions regarding poverty in Africa should embrace the idea of spirituality. The concept of spirituality will appeal to a wider audience irrespective of religious affiliation or the lack of it since agnostics can have some spiritual traits as well. Our target audiences for this paper are policy makers, SME operators, would-be entrepreneurs, policy makers, international donors and scholars concerned with poverty on the continent. It is perhaps important to emphasize that our use of the concept of spirituality in this paper does not relate to the supernatural, to God or religion. Instead, we used the literature on spiritual intelligence (Emmons, 1998; 1999; 2000; Gardner, 1993; 1995; 1997; Kwilecki, 1988) to identify key spiritual traits that can enhance policy making and business operation.

4.2 Spirituality, Policy Formulation and SME Management

Spirituality: experts on spirituality have argued that people who are spiritual demonstrate ultimate concern through personal striving for goal (Apter, 1985; Emmons, 1999; Jaworski, 1996; Pargament & Park, 1995). These concerns in a nutshell refer to the meaning of life; what one finds meaningful as well as the search for what is meaningful in whatever one does. Thus, spiritual people in any life endeavour have the goal of finding meaning in what they do. They are motivated by the search for meaning which encourages them to take action. They also derive satisfaction from goal attainment. This implies that if spiritual impoverishment can be removed from people, especially public office holders and business operators, then it is possible to make a significant improvement in poverty reduction and underdevelopment. Although *material poverty* (i.e. income, education and health) has been the main concern of policy makers and international development agencies, *spiritual poverty* which can be a catalyst for material poverty is hardly acknowledged or pursued actively. Figure 4-1 below illustrates our argument that the main cause of material poverty is spiritual impoverishment which leads to undesirable behaviour that creates and perpetuates poverty. This spiritual impoverishment is not only restricted to politicians, public servants, policy makers and SME operators. The victims (the poor) can also suffer from spiritual impoverishment by condoning or encouraging the rent-seeking behaviour of the privileged few under the guise of tribalism, regionalism or religiosity.

Figure 4-1. The Chain of Poverty in Africa

Even when *educational poverty* is acknowledged and pursued, the aim is to use the outcomes for material ends. Therefore, educational curricula are devoid of the spiritual dimension. The link between *spiritual poverty* and material poverty will be elaborated later. The chapter argues that unless this link is appreciated and integrated in the thinking behind policy formulation and implementation in the fight against poverty in Africa, a sustainable outcome is likely to be a dream. This is because spirituality has the potential to appeal to the senses of any African irrespective of ethnicity, religion, social class or level of education. Also, the implementers of policy and the target (i.e. the poor and the SME operators) need to appreciate the imperative of broader concerns beyond personal material poverty. Indeed Emmons (2009: 4) pointed out:

> .... It is, therefore, ultimate concern that shapes and gives direction to a person's ultimate concerns in life. Spiritual strivings, then, as personal goals focused on the sacred, become the way in which ultimate concerns

are encountered in people's lives. Ultimate concerns are bridges linking motivation, spirituality, and intelligence.

Given that the meaning of what people do as a vocation can be a motivator and satisfier, it is imperative that SME operators and policy makers identify the ultimate meaning in what they do beyond the means of earning a livelihood. Thus, African policy makers and public office holders should have in their education and staff development curricula, a spiritual dimension to the essence of public service and policy formulation and implementation. *By that we explicitly mean deriving something meaningful through understanding and appreciating the impact of their action on themselves and the wider society.* Similarly, SME development and training for potential entrepreneurs should involve understanding and appreciating the "business benefits" of adopting the "spiritual" approach to setting up and running a business in the African context. These arguments are elaborated in the following sections focusing on spiritual traits and system thinking.

4.3 Spiritual Traits and their Practical Implications

Writers on spiritual intelligence have argued that some people have certain characteristics, call them spiritual traits that enable them to not only find an overall satisfaction in life but also influence others significantly in the process (Emmons, 1998; 1999; 2000; Gardner, 1993; 1995; 1997; Kwilecki, 1988). For the purpose of this paper which focuses on poverty reduction, identifying such people or developing them should make a significant contribution to the fight against poverty in Africa. If a critical mass of such people can be developed in key sectors of the economy and the governance system, appropriate policies can be enacted and implemented effectively given that such people would be deriving personal satisfaction from the effective implementation of such policy rather than engaging in rent-seeking behaviour which has been the major cause of policy failures in Africa and developing countries. Therefore, spiritual traits amongst policy makers, public servants and business operators can have significant practical potential for the fight against poverty and underdevelopment on the African continent. The potential can be gleaned from the following statements:

At a minimum, spiritually intelligent individuals are characterized by (a) the capacity for transcendence; (b) the ability to enter into heightened spiritual states of consciousness; (c) the ability to invest everyday activities, events, and relationships with a sense of the sacred; (d) the ability to utilize spiritual resources to solve problems in living; and (e) the capacity to engage in virtuous behaviour or to be virtuous. (Emmons, 2000: 10)

The following sections discuss three of the five components of spiritual traits as they relate to policy making and the management of SMEs within the context of poverty reduction in Africa. These traits have direct practical implications for policy formulation and business management. Therefore, policy makers and SME operators can benefit from being sensitised regarding the positive impact that such traits can have on policy formulation and implementation as well as on running a successful business which can lead to poverty reduction.

Transcending the Material: One important component of spiritual traits is the ability to transcend the physical and the material (Emmons, 2000; Slife, Hope, & Nebeker, 1997). According to the experts (Emmons, 2000; Piedmont, 1999), transcendence is the capacity of a person to sense a synchronicity to life and to develop a bond with humanity. Referring to several authors (Piedmont, 1999; Walsh & Vaughan, 1993) Emmons (2000: 10) points out that transcendence "has been viewed 'as an art' capable of developing capacities of the mind such as attentional training and refining awareness". From the practical point of view, transcendence should enable people to develop a strong bond with humanity rather than with their own tribe, religion, race or nationality. *Transcendent* people derive pleasure and satisfaction not from material acquisition or achievements but from the sense of rising above such acquisitions and achievements (Dyer, 2007). In other words, the sense of satisfaction can come from giving away material, for example. This is not to suggest that people with spiritual traits do not or should not be involved in material acquisition. On the contrary, many are deeply engaged in economic activities. However, they are usually involved in such activities to make a difference in society. The strong bond with humanity enables them to have a wider perspective of the purpose of economic activity which leads to behaviours devoid of exclusive attachment to sectional interests such as race, tribe and religion. This might not be the initial objective at the early stage of their *journey*, but towards the end, through psychological maturity (Feinstein & Krippner, 1988; Fowler, 1981, Seaward, 1995), they develop a sense of satisfaction from transcending the material and the physical. Philanthropists are extremely rich people in their own societies. Many if not most are spiritual in their outlook and their purpose. Within the context of poverty reduction in Africa, developing and using people with spiritual traits in the public and the private sectors should make a significant difference in the fight against poverty and underdevelopment.

The Application of Transcendent Traits in Business and Policy Making: This spiritual trait (i.e. Transcendence) should be used in all poverty reduction interventions targeting SMEs and policy making. For example, training and development programs on entrepreneurship as well as public policy making should have a specific section that advocates the virtues of greater purpose (non-material) for the business (i.e. SME). Similarly, poverty reduction policy formulation should not be focused only on material poverty given that spiritual poverty can be the main cause of material poverty. Technical skills related to policy making or running a business should be anchored to the greater purpose (e.g. societal development). People should know why the skills are important to them and the wider society and most importantly perhaps, how the skills can contribute to the eradication of poverty. Assessment and recognition of achievements should be anchored to greater purpose as well. Trainees should be made aware from the outset that the business (i.e. SME) or public policy should be a means to a greater purpose than an end in itself. SMEs' operators and prospective entrepreneurs should be provided with practical examples and cases which demonstrate how bonding with humanity at large rather than a sectional interest makes business sense. Governments and International Development Interventions should recognize and reward policy makers and SMEs who demonstrate a sustainable capacity to transcend material achievements. In other words, SME success should not only be measured in terms of revenue or profit, but also on employment generation and the wellbeing of workers. These principles advocated in this section provide a guide that should be applied to all facets of SME development and policy making. SME operators should also be encouraged to imbibe such principles in their daily operations.

Sanctification of Daily Activities: The notion of sanctification is one of the important and relevant spiritual traits that should make a significant impact on the behaviour of policy makers and business operators within the context of poverty reduction in Africa. This concept provides the further means of putting the concept of transcendence into practice in the daily activities of policy makers, public office holders and SME operators. What does sanctification mean? According to Emmons (2000: 11) "To *sanctify*, means to set apart for a special purpose". In other words, there should be a greater and broader purpose even in the mundane minute activities. This concept should appeal to the followers of the two main religions in Africa (Christianity and Islam). For example, in Islam, worship (*Ibadah*) is not only the rituals such as praying and fasting, but whatever a *muslim* does "appropriately" is also worship. This means that the sanctification of policy making activities or the conducting of daily business activities should take a different dimension in the minds of policy makers and SME operators. They should be fully conscious of the wider implications on society of their daily activities since spiritually endowed people bond with humanity at large rather than a sectional interest. In fact, it has been argued that through sanctification people see the divine even in ordinary activities (Monk et al., 1998). Similarly, the work people do should be seen as a calling rather than a vocation (Davidson & Caddell, 1994; Emmons, 2000; Novak, 1996). According to Emmons, Cheung, and Tehrani (1998), when work is spiritualised through sanctification, people become "imbued with a sense of the sacred, these goals take on a significance and power not found in secular strivings" (Emmons, 2000: 12). Undoubtedly, within the African context where religion is revered, leveraging the notion of sanctification to change the attitudes and behaviour of policy makers and business operators should appeal to all concerned. The spiritualisation of daily activities through sanctification should not be difficult as the dominant religions on the continent (Christianity and Islam) advocate the use of daily endeavours to achieve the greater good and salvation. Both religions advocate the application of the scriptures in daily activities (Emmons et al., 1998; 1999). However, the only problem in the African context is that such teachings are applied exclusively rather than inclusively. This is the main reason for the choice of spirituality rather than religion as a means of contextualizing the fight against poverty in Africa.

The Application of Sanctification in Business and Policy Making: This spiritual trait (i.e. the Sanctification of Daily Activities) should not be difficult to comprehend since followers of the two major religions are expected to sanctify their daily actions. If that is the case, a legitimate question to ask is why are they not doing it? Part of the answer to this question is the lack of learning transfer. Irrespective of religious affiliation, many followers of the two religions are unable to transfer the teaching of their scriptures into their offices and business. This is largely because of the de-contextualization of the professional training of public office holders and business curricula. Another reason is the exclusive interpretation of the teachings. These two factors have been having a devastating impact on social and economic development leading to the current social conflicts and rampant poverty on the continent. Now that there is clear evidence that such an approach is not working (i.e. the de-contextualization of interventions), there is an urgent need to integrate the socio-cultural context of Africans in any development initiatives. The operators of the so-called modern sector who find solace and nourishment in the socio-cultural traditions of Africa in their hour of need but behave in a contrary fashion when operating in their public offices and businesses, should be sensitised to sanctify their daily activities. The sensitisation initiative should take an instrumental approach rather than an altruistic approach. This means that public office holders/policy makers and SME operators should be provided with clear evidence of the material and non-material benefits of sanctifying their daily activities. There are several practical personal development materials, books and case studies that can help achieve this objective.

Virtuous Behaviour: Spiritually endowed people demonstrate virtuous behaviour on a consistent basis. According to Emmons (2000), such people show forgiveness, express gratitude, exhibit humility and compassion, and display sacrificial love. Another important element of virtuous behaviour which we believe is critical to success in the fight against poverty in Africa is self-control. According to Baumeister and Exline (1999) self-control is at the heart of success in every human endeavour. Self-control or the lack of it is a significant determinant of other human limitations such as anger, pride, greed, lust and envy. *Control these and you are on your way to success* suggests the perennial philosophy. Emmons (2000: 13) also pointed out that

> ...Virtues connect to both motivation, representing ultimate concerns, and to effective action. Conceiving of these inner qualities as virtues, implies that these are sources of human strength that enable people to function effectively in the world.

Virtues are so important to the point that some writers argue that they are the closest characteristic of a person that defines who (s)he is (Zagzebski, 1996). The good news is that virtues can be acquired. As Zagzebski (1996) pointed out, virtues are acquired excellences of the person. Good virtues have universal application. No culture or religion or race has a monopoly on good virtues. This makes it easier to advocate the inculcation of good virtues amongst public office holders and SME operators. The challenge however is to preach virtue to those who are spiritually impoverished. Such people would appreciate the benefits and application of good virtues but only to their inner circle (e.g. religious affiliation, social class affiliation, racial or tribal affiliation). Virtuous behaviour should be the manifestation of the first two spiritual traits discussed above. Virtuous behaviour is significantly compatible with the fight against poverty. Both policy makers and SME operators can make a significant contribution to poverty reduction if they behave in a virtuous manner. Indeed, most successful business people demonstrate such traits because to do so makes business sense. For example, successful business people hire the best employee irrespective of race and sectarian affiliation because it makes business sense to do so. Not to do so is to commit business or professional suicide. Successful business people are colour blind and are bonded with humanity as a philosophy and strategy for business. In depth analysis of the vision and mission statements of successful companies would reveal spirituality in action. Such mission statements are devoid of any aspect of exclusion and sectionalism.

The Application of Virtuous Behaviour in Business and Policy Making: This spiritual trait (i.e. Virtuous Behaviour) should be universally applauded when policy makers and SME operators demonstrate it in their daily activities. Therefore it should be integrated into policy formulation and implementation. However, within the context of poverty reduction in Africa, the virtuous behaviour that should be emphasized the most is self-control. This is because self-control is more directly relevant to policy making and implementation. Also, SME operators and prospective entrepreneurs would find self-discipline to be the cornerstone of business success. Another reason for the need to emphasize self-control as a virtuous behaviour is that it directly influences the effective application of other virtuous behaviours. For example, a business person should know how to apply compassion otherwise he/she will lose the business in a society ravaged by poverty. Similarly, policy makers and implementers (e.g. law enforcers) need to know how and when to apply compassion otherwise the policies will be toothless and in the end create even more poverty. In an African culture where "people are their brothers' keeper" compassion is highly valued but gradually misused leading to ineffective policy implementation and poor service delivery. The approach for instilling virtuous behaviour through self-control is not to preach the ills of compassion for example, but rather to demonstrate the benefits of making effective decisions on when and how to be compassionate regarding the formulation and/or implementation of policies. Psychologists have indicated that almost all behaviours are learned. They can also be unlearned. There are practical tools that can help in the development and sustenance of any "good" behaviour. Such tools should be part of the initiatives for poverty reduction policies and implementation as they relate to public servants and SME operators. Using psychological tools, people can be shown how to remove bad habits and replace them with good ones. In a nutshell, there are tools that can help develop virtuous behaviour. Programmes like Neuro-Linguistic programming can help business people and policy makers change the way they think, leading to a positive change in behaviour.

4.4 System Theory as a Foundation for Policy Making and SME Management

To the neutral observer, system theory provides a further explanation for the potency of spirituality in addressing the challenge of poverty in Africa. System theory is not a substitute for spirituality but it is complementary. The former is secular and neutral in all intents and purposes. The latter, although carrying out an almost identical function, is value-laden and "emotional". It can be argued that system theory is the *scientific version* of the practical dimensions of spirituality. The approach of system thinking is fundamentally different from the traditional form of analysing a social phenomenon. While the latter is focused on breaking the system and studying its constituent parts separately, the former focuses on studying the constituent parts in relation to others. For example, poverty is part of a system in the sense that it is an outcome of certain behaviours, and functions of some sub-systems, social and economic structures, etc. Therefore, a system theorist would argue that in order to understand and address poverty, it is necessary to study poverty within the system in which poverty emerged, hence the socio-cultural focus adopted by this book. We argue that most approaches to dealing with poverty and SME development are based on traditional forms of analyses where the issues are not tackled from multiple angles but from a specific disciplinary perspective. Our approach takes a multi-disciplinary "system" perspective. However, to achieve this objective we faced the challenge of finding an appropriate concept that will be equally *understandable, comprehensible, applicable* and, *relevant* to policy makers, SME operators, trainers and trainees. The following section provides a summary of system thinking and its application within the context of poverty reduction. We then integrate spirituality with system thinking to come up with frameworks on how material poverty is produced and reproduced by what we call *spiritual poverty*. At the end of reading the two sections, the reader will hopefully appreciate the uncanny resemblance between spirituality (practically speaking) and system thinking.

4.5 System Thinking and its Application in Poverty Reduction, Policy Formulation and SME Management

What is a system and what is system thinking? How does system thinking relate to the idea of SMEs for poverty reduction or a policy for poverty reduction? Experts argue that to qualify as a system, a unit should be composed of interrelated parts that cooperate in a specific process or processes that have a purpose (Boulding, 1956). It is of course not every operator in a system who is aware of the purpose of the system. However, in a social system such as a government or business organization, the failure to appreciate the purpose of a system can be fatal to the existence of the system (Banathy, 1996). This is because a lack of knowledge of the purpose can lead to independent behavior (i.e. a lack of cooperation).

In system thinking, problems are viewed as part of an overall system rather than a unique independent event, occurrence or outcome (Banathy, 1991). Most importantly perhaps, such an event or occurrence is analyzed within the context of its potential future consequences on other systems as well as within the system where the event occurred. It is important to emphasize that system thinking is not just "thinking" but also behaviour, habit and practice. In a nutshell, system thinking is a state of mind that needs to be developed by policy makers and SME operators in order to achieve the goal of poverty reduction. In fact, effective policy making and strategic management rest on the foundation of system thinking. A good strategic plan must take the overall organizational internal and external systems into account. Similarly, a good policy on SMEs and poverty reduction should be based on the careful analysis of the multiple social and economic systems and how they might enable or constrain the implementation of the policy. This is because systems interact to produce specific outcomes. Policies should not be developed in a vacuum without scenario planning and consultation with relevant stakeholders as well as relevant disciplines.

An SME and a government policy department are systems that are made up of many components in the process of producing outputs (goods, services, and policies). They are also part of a wider system (i.e. a governance structure, or economic and social systems). In order for the internal system of the department and the SME to function effectively, all the constituent parts have to cooperate with each other and with the wider systems. One way to manifest this cooperation is to show concern and act for the effective functioning of the social system. More specifically, in the African context, to show wider concern means to be concerned with poverty and underdevelopment. The idea of concern is also echoed in the explanation of spirituality (Apter, 1985; Emmons, 1999; 2009; Jaworski, 1996; Pargament & Park, 1995). However, this concern by the state department/unit and the SME is not for altruistic reasons but for survival as a system given that systems do not operate in a vacuum. The existence of one system can depend on the existence of the wider systems. The concept of a *failed state* is a case in point. Appreciation of this basic fact is central to system thinking when dealing with policy formulation on poverty and good governance in general.

Since normal people think before they act, *system thinking* assumes that for a system to operate effectively, the operators of the system need to think and act in a systemic way (Banathy, 1991; Checkland, 1981). Therefore, for SMEs to contribute to poverty reduction, SME operators and policy makers must think and act in a systemic way. Thus, SMEs and policy makers must think and act in relation to the social and economic systems and not based on narrow selfish interests. This is another area where spirituality overlaps with system thinking. System thinking has been used by many experts across many disciplines to refer to the understanding of systems' behaviour and their interaction with other systems in the wider environment (Checkland, 1981). System thinking is largely referring to as an approach to problem solving regarding social systems such as business organizations and governments (Checkland, 1981; Flood & Jackson, 1991). By problem we mean–how are any issues requiring attention actually tackled. For example, poverty is an issue of social and economic development that requires urgent attention. This problem would require system thinking to understand the complexity of poverty and its multi-faceted nature. Using system thinking we can understand from the "external" as well as the "personal" perspectives of the complexity of poverty. A lot has been written about the "external" nature of poverty. Experts have talked about the causes of poverty which are generally from the "external" perspective. These include poor governance, bad policies, the environment, conflict, etc. Using a system approach we argue that "external" factors collaborate with "personal" factors (e.g. *spiritual impoverishment*) to produce the nature and extent of poverty. This is because, from a system perspective, no unit, factor or even sub-system operates in a vacuum (Bateson, 1979). The *personal* perspective to poverty is the individual himself/herself. Social psychologists have demonstrated that individuals react to their circumstances in different ways leading to different outcomes (Hofstede, 1991). This is a classic case of system behaviour. Thus, the individual (i.e. a system or unit) is interacting with the circumstances (i.e. another unit or system) to produce an outcome (i.e. poverty). Figure 4-2 below illustrates our point.

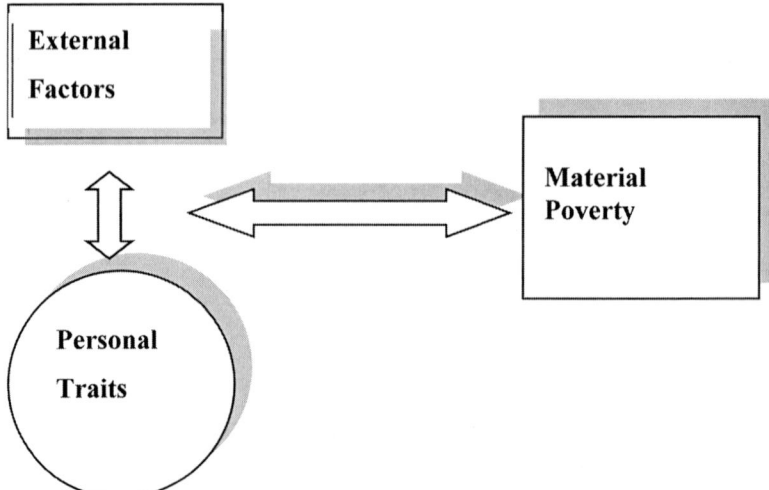

Figure 4-2. How poverty is produced and reproduced using System Theory

What constitutes the "personal" perspective of poverty? There are many elements that constitute this perspective to poverty. For our purpose we focus on the spiritual dimensions. This section introduces the concept of "Spiritual Poverty" as a "personal" cause of poverty in others and also a "state" of poverty in oneself. Based on the literature reviewed in the previous sections, we came up with a profile of a spiritually poor person. Practically speaking, to be spiritually poor is to:

1. fail to understand that one's action will affect others which will in turn impact on one's well being;
2. lack self-contentment and self-control;
3. lack the ability to see the wider common interest;
4. lack the ability to delay gratification;
5. lack the ability to see positive potential in human beings irrespective of their backgrounds;
6. lack the ability to focus on true personal development and growth;
7. focus too narrowly on self, religion, race, tribe, region and nation rather than humanity.

As depicted in figure 4-3, these "personal" factors on their own or in collaboration with other "external" factors create poverty in others through egotistical decisions and rent-seeking behaviour in policy making, policy implementation and business management. Spiritual poverty leads to a state of fear, anger and envy which also leads to undesirable behaviour and consequences. For example, corruption by public office holders is caused by a lack of self-control and self-contentment which leads to the material impoverishment of others and oneself in the long run.

We argue that the above seven elements of spiritual poverty can be the basis for developing personal development programmes for policy makers, relevant public servants and SME operators. The African socio-cultural context programmes with strong foundations in psychology and spirituality can be appealing to participants. Similarly, personal development materials such as Covey's seminal book, *Seven Habits of Highly Effective People* should be part of the recommended reading. For the SME operators' a "must-read" material is Napoleon Hill's book *Think and Grow Rich*. This classic offers a spiritual dimension to running a successful business that benefits society. Other recommended reading for SME operators and relevant public servants are the biographies of Nelson Mandela and John D. Rockefeller. The essence of diagrams 4-1, 4-2 and 4-3 is to emphasize that tackling poverty in Africa requires a two-prong approach. One approach should deal with the "external" causes of poverty, and this approach is being pursued by governments, international agencies and even non-government organizations and private individuals. The other approach which is either not recognized or ignored is the "personal" approach. Both the poor and those with the potential to help eradicate poverty (e.g. SME operators and policy makers) should be subjected to the sensitisation of the personal and societal benefits of the spiritual approach advocated in this chapter.

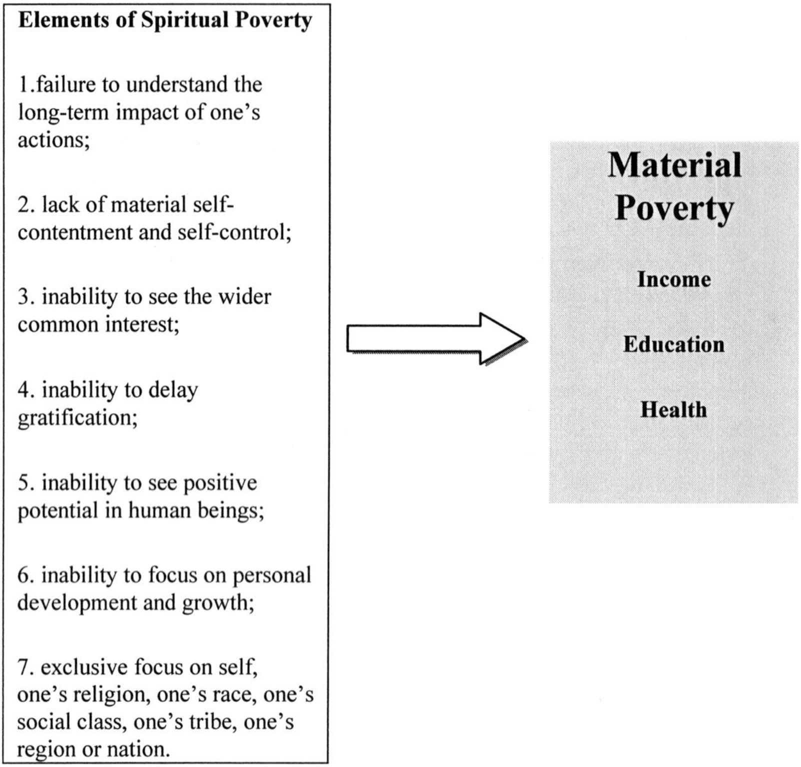

Elements of Spiritual Poverty

1. failure to understand the long-term impact of one's actions;

2. lack of material self-contentment and self-control;

3. inability to see the wider common interest;

4. inability to delay gratification;

5. inability to see positive potential in human beings;

6. inability to focus on personal development and growth;

7. exclusive focus on self, one's religion, one's race, one's social class, one's tribe, one's region or nation.

Material Poverty

Income

Education

Health

Figure 4-3. How Material Poverty is caused by Spiritual Poverty

4.6 Conclusion

This chapter set out to provide another perspective for dealing with poverty on the African continent. We argue that African poverty and ways to address it must take a novel approach rather than be focused exclusively on material poverty which leads to the prescription of the same medicine that has proven to be ineffective over the years. In others words, technical training on policy making or the provision of courses on setting up and running a business with some financial support is not enough to enable the private sector to address the enormous challenges of poverty on the continent. The novel approach advocated in the chapter is the broadening of the conceptualization of poverty to include spiritual poverty. In fact, we argue that spiritual poverty is a main cause of material poverty. Therefore, we used the literature on spiritual intelligence to identify spiritual traits that can be developed to enable policy makers, public servants and business operators in Africa to think and behave "appropriately" in the fight against poverty. We also used system theory to complement the concept of spirituality in demonstrating the need for a holistic approach at individual, business and governmental levels when dealing with,poverty reduction in Africa. We also provided indicative guidelines and principles for the development of policy makers, relevant public servants, SME operators and would-be entrepreneurs.

CHAPTER FIVE

PERSONAL DEVELOPMENT OF THE POOR AND THE ENTREPRENEURS

5.1 Introduction

In the previous chapter, we discussed various issues regarding poverty in Africa and how SMEs can help in eradicating poverty. We also alluded to the fact that states and international donors and institutions have invested significantly in training entrepreneurs with the aim of reducing unemployment, especially amongst young people. Almost all of the training interventions provided to would-be entrepreneurs in Africa are based on the assumption that trainees will be successful if they are provided with the practical skills for running a business. The main argument advanced in this chapter is that skills-training is the wrong place to start the intervention. This is because not every unemployed person should be encouraged to start a business. The reason for this assertion will become clear at the end of the chapter. Our approach to training intervention is guided by the following statement made by Stephen Covey in his ground-breaking book, *"The 7 Habits of Highly Effective People."* The author argued,

> Sow a thought, reap an action, sow an action, reap a habit, sow a habit, reap a character, sow a character, and reap a destiny.

In a nutshell, for training to be effective and to make a lasting impact on would-be entrepreneurs, it has to start with the mind, i.e. re-orientation. By using the central theme of this book "Spiritual Poverty," this chapter will draw on the works of renowned personnel development "Gurus" such as Stephen Covey, Brian Tracy and Wayne Dyer, to suggest the critical foundation of training would-be entrepreneurs in Africa. The chapter will discuss the concept and context of success for the entrepreneur; the importance of purpose, beliefs and values; the understanding of an individual's strengths and weaknesses; the setting of personal goals and how to achieve them; and finally, determining the critical habits that will deliver success. All of these issues will be discussed within the context of SMEs and poverty reduction in Africa.

5.2 What is Success?

Living a successful life requires an understanding of the meaning of success. Success should be the basis of setting a goal for living. Unfortunately, entrepreneurship training programs do not usually consider the articulation of success as a key element in a training intervention. Within the context of poverty reduction in Africa, trainers should help trainees first understand what it is they are seeking by setting up a business. This is important because it is likely that other avenues rather than the setting up a business might be more viable options for them, especially if they do not have the qualities to run a successful business. What then should be considered success? In other words, how would a person know that he/she is successful? Within the context of spiritual poverty or spiritual endowment, success is not about material acquisition or power. This might not sound convincing to the poor and unemployed person who can hardly afford the basics things in life. Nonetheless, this is the hard truth that is unavoidable. The major task of the trainers is to drive home this fact in the initial stage of the training programme. Brian Tracey (1995), in his best-selling book, "*Maximum Achievement: Strategies and Skills that will Unlock your Hidden Powers to Succeed*," identified seven ingredients of success in life. These are what all normal people seek in life and define their essence of being human. Although the author did not categorize them in any order, for the sake of simplicity during training, we encourage the trainers to consider *Peace of mind* as the most important factor that defines success. Peace of mind is another way of describing *happiness*. True happiness or peace of mind can be achieved through material or non-material acquisition. In other words, if people can be reoriented to understand that they can reach the same destination through various routes, it will be easier to sift through the unemployed and provide them with the means of livelihood through targeted and specific intervention, rather than lumping them all in entrepreneurship training programmes.

According to Brian Tracy (1993: 23),

> *The wonderful truth about peace of mind is that it is your normal natural condition. Happiness is your birth right. It belongs to you. It is not something you experience occasionally if you're lucky. Peace of mind is central to your existence. It's the basic precondition for enjoying everything else.*

These statements clearly suggest that all human beings are striving for one simple thing: peace of mind. They pursue various routes to achieve it. However, many are not aware of the several routes available to them. Many could not distinguish the map from the territory. The territory is the peace of mind while the map is the means. The main task of the trainer is to help the trainees appreciate the difference. The pursuit of material acquisition without focus on the territory is the reason why in Africa, many people focus on material acquisition, leading to undesirable behaviour that destroys the territory (i.e. peace of mind). In the previous chapters, we demonstrated that spiritually endowed people are connected to the environment within which they operate. They understand that their peace of mind depends on the peace of mind of others. People suffering from spiritual poverty think they can cut corners and achieve peace of mind through non virtuous behaviours such as denying people their rights, selling inferior products, looting public funds, and extorting the poor and the under-privileged. Evidence indicates that such people never achieve a sustainable peace of mind, even if they appear to be happy.

Therefore, to be successful is to achieve peace of mind. The amazing thing about peace of mind is that once it is achieved, its value is equal to everyone else's. Unlike material acquisition that can be quantified with some people having more than others, peace of mind cannot be quantified. You either have it or you do not. It is nature's way of levelling the playing field for all. If the trainers are able to impress on the trainees the concept of success derived from peace of mind, the next step in the training intervention is to determine how to achieve this through running a business or doing something else. The thrust of the argument for achieving peace of mind is that while achieving peace of mind is the ultimate goal, and the sole means of measuring the achievement of personal success, it cannot be achieved without consideration for others. In other words, trainers should emphasize the need for trainees to be interdependent rather than independent. The naked pursuit of independence by SME operators and public office holders is responsible for the degradation of the social fabric of society, leading to rampant poverty. The imperative of interdependence is aptly captured by Stephen Covey's statements in his classic book, "*The 7 Habits of Highly Effective People.*"

> Life is, by nature, highly interdependent. To try to achieve maximum effectiveness through interdependence is like trying to play tennis with a golf club–the tool is not suited for reality. Interdependence is a far more mature, more advanced concept. If I am physically interdependent, I am self-reliant and capable, but I also realize that you and I working together can accomplish far more than even my best that I could accomplish alone.

If I am emotionally interdependent, I derive a great sense of worth within myself, but also recognise the need for love, for giving, and for receiving love from others. If I am intellectually interdependent, I realize that I need the best thinking of other people to join with my own.

The concept of interdependence is in tune with the notions of spirituality and system thinking discussed in the previous chapters. The three concepts are the foundation and bedrock of building sustainable peace of mind upon which success is determined and measured.

Activity

How can trainers put the idea of measuring success into practice during training intervention? One way of developing an in-class activity to help trainees appreciate how to measure their success within the context of poverty reduction is to first ask them (1) if they had the choice, would they be starting up their own business? If not, ask them what they would rather be doing? (2) The next step is to ask them what they hope to achieve by pursuing this endeavour; (3) The third question, ask them how they would know if their pursuit is successful? The answers to these questions should lead to the discussion and determination of the extent to which they understand, appreciate, and embrace the notion of the ultimate goal in life (happiness), spiritual endowment, interdependence, and system thinking.

Both the aim and purpose of this activity are to help the trainees appreciate that there should be a broader perspective on setting up a business.

5.2.1 Other Ways to Measure Success in Life

In the previous section we demonstrated that the ultimate criterion of success is peace of mind or happiness. Other measures of success in life also matter. These are all tied to peace of mind, or to put it another way, they contribute to peace of mind. Some are the foundation of achievement. For example, the concept of *Health and Energy* is one of the measures or goals of a successful life, without which there will be no peace of mind. Would-be entrepreneurs should be sensitised about the importance of health and energy, because in the pursuit of short-term monetary goals, SME operators have been known to jeopardise their health through working excessively hard or taking harmful drugs to boost their energy. Within the African context where many still believe in traditional fortune tellers, quack doctors, and cultist movements, there is a great need to drive home the importance of the concept of *health and energy* as a worthy goal to be pursued by the entrepreneur. This task will be harder if the trainees are mainly young people who are normally healthy and have yet to experience the negative effects of poor health. Besides, it is hard to make a poor unemployed youth focus on health rather than money. However, if the concept of health and energy is demonstrated to be a strong tool for running a successful business, even the young and healthy will appreciate the importance of health and energy as a criterion for measuring success. What is the point of making money only for it to be used for paying hospital bills? In other words, a businessman who works himself into the hospital can hardly be described as a successful businessman.

Human beings are social animals. This is more so in the African context. The inherent interdependence amongst African people, partly due to culture and partly due to the absence of effective institutions and public service demands that *relationship* is an important criterion for measuring the success of a business operator. The relationship criterion is multi-faceted. It starts with domestic or family relationships, moves to commercial relationships, and culminates in community relationships. There are economic benefits for building effective relationships across the three dimensions of the relationships. It is imperative that the trainees are sensitised about the benefits of an effective family and commercial and community relationships as key factors for developing a successful business venture.

The fourth factor that should be considered as a criterion for measuring success in life is *financial freedom*. Note that we are not talking about the quantity of money, but freedom from being dependent on other people in order to satisfy what a person needs to live a comfortable life. Financial freedom is certainly an important factor that can contribute to the ultimate goal in life–which is peace of mind. However, financial freedom is not the only factor. In fact, financial freedom cannot guarantee happiness–i.e. peace of mind. Entrepreneurship training programmes should bring into focus not only the financial performance of the business, but the financial freedom that the business will provide to the SME operator. Hence, the measure of success for the SME operator is not the amount of money generated by the business, but the financial freedom that the business provides to the business operator. A business owner can generate one million dollars' profit, but will have less freedom financially than another business owner whose business generates ten thousand dollars. Such examples should help to develop a clear perspective to trainees that the business is a means, not an end. However, this is not to suggest that trainees should not set high financial targets for their businesses. On the contrary, trainees should be encouraged to continuously improve through setting higher and achievable targets across all areas of their operation, provided that they do so within the contexts of system thinking, spirituality, and interdependence. It is only through this approach that they will be successful in poverty reduction and in achieving sustainable peace of mind.

The fifth factor that can make a significant contribution to happiness and act as a criterion for measuring success is the pursuit of *worthy goals and ideals*. There is no better way to explain this than to quote Brian Tracy himself (1993: 29). According to the author:

> To be truly happy, you need a clear sense of direction. You need a commitment to something bigger and more important than yourself. You need to feel that your life stands for something; that you are somehow making a valuable contribution to your world.

These statements are clearly in tune with the concept of spirituality discussed in the previous chapters. The statements suggest that virtuous acts are not necessarily selfless acts, but behaviours guided by enlightened self-interest. In fact, the author defined happiness as *"the progressive realization of a worthy ideal."* This suggests that the pursuit of worthy ideals would lead to the ultimate goal in life. Where does entrepreneurship training fit into this?

First, trainees should be made aware that setting up and running a successful business is a worthy goal that can improve their livelihood and that of others. Second, the trainees should be re-oriented to see the business as a means of helping the community to access goods and services, and above all, a means of eradicating poverty through job creation. A simple exercise that can help bring these ideas to life is to ask the trainees to write a list of ways their businesses can help their communities rather than ways the businesses can help them. Or, in order to identify the categories of trainees, the trainer can start by asking them to fill in the following table.

Table 5-1: How the business can help

How The Business Can Help Me	How The Business Can Help My Community
1.	1.
2.	2.
3.	3.
4.	4.
5.	5.

The sixth factor that can be a significant contributor to happiness and peace of mind and is therefore a measure of success is *self-knowledge*. In fact, successful business people are characterized by self-awareness. They know their strengths and weaknesses. Researchers have also found that successful entrepreneurs have specific qualities that ensure their success. Training programs should be designed with self-knowledge as the core of the intervention. As Brian Tracy (1993: 30) points out:

> To perform at your best, you need to know who you are, and why you think and feel the way you do. You need to understand the forces and influences that have shaped your character from earliest childhood. You need to know why you react and respond the way you do to people and situations around you.

The issue of self-awareness is vital in any entrepreneurship training program. The quick-fix approach to addressing youth unemployment through funding people to set up businesses requires a total overhaul. Governments in Africa must accept the reality that not all of the unemployed can run a sustainable business. No amount of training can turn some people into successful entrepreneurs. Similarly, the unemployed themselves should face reality. For some, attempting to set up and run a business might be the last option available to them. They will not know that unless they undertake a self-diagnosis of their own qualities and capabilities within the context of entrepreneurship.

> ***Activity***
>
> A good training programme should start with a needs analysis. Trainees should be provided with psychometric instruments to assess their personalities, such as their spiritual, emotional and business intelligence. Further qualitative approaches can also be used for self-diagnosis. These should be the basis for setting a personal development goal for each trainee. It may well be that after the exercise, some trainees might opt for a different career or refocus their attention from becoming a sole operator of a business to a partner. The trainers should use the outcome of the self-diagnosis to guide the trainees on pursuing the ultimate goal i.e. peace of mind. This might be through setting up a business or being employed by another business owner. The choice of business should be influenced by the characteristics of the person.

The final determinant of peace of mind is *personal fulfilment*. According to Brian Tracy (1993: 17),

> *this is a feeling that you are becoming everything that you are capable of becoming. It is the sure knowledge that you are moving toward the realization of your full potential as a human being.*

Obviously, from the training point of view, the criterion of measuring success is more of a journey than a destination. For some trainees, the fact that they are part of a training programme is in itself an achievement that can demonstrate the journey towards the realization of their dreams. However, the key point to emphasize here is that trainees should appreciate that there is something called "self-actualization," or self-fulfilment. This comes first by having a worthy ambition. If the ambition is not worthy, its achievement will not deliver sustainable happiness.

We conclude this section by presenting a brief summary of Wayne Dyer's book, "The 10 Secrets for Success and Inner Peace." The ten secrets are:

- Have a mind that is open to everything and attached to nothing;
- Don't die with your music still in you;
- You can't give away what you don't have;
- Embrace silence. (Tough task in some cultures);
- Give up your personal history;
- You can't solve a problem with the same mind that created it;
- There are no justified resentments;
- Treat yourself as if you are already what you want to be;
- Treasure your divinity;
- Wisdom is avoiding all thoughts that weaken you. (Dyer, W., 2001)

5.2.2 Helping Trainees to Examine their Values and Beliefs

Having determined the definition of success, the would-be entrepreneurs need to turn their attention on themselves. To put it bluntly, there is no point going through an entrepreneurship training programme without clear answers to: (1) what do you want in life? (2) why do you want it? 3) what can you do with it when you get it? These three questions are key factors in understanding each trainee and their potential regarding why they are where they are and what can be done to help them. Also, the answers to these questions should help to determine their potential for poverty reduction, should they succeed in setting up their own businesses. So where do we start?

5.2.3 Understanding Trainees' Values

The starting point is the determination of the values of trainees. Basically, values guide a person in distinguishing what is right and what is wrong. More broadly, values help people to choose how they want to live their lives. They guide people in making big decisions that will have a long-term impact on the way they live. Given that values are acquired from childhood and reinforced by societal traditions, we do not always examine our values. In fact, until we are confronted by major issues in life or asked directly, most of us do not even think we have values or are guided by them. A typical person thinks his/her choices are guided by objective and rational factors. Therefore, in a training program that is aimed at changing the condition of people, it is critical that trainees are confronted with the key question pertaining to their values. There should be a clear determination of what they consider important in life. Trainees should be asked to examine their values and how they want to live their lives. As the saying goes, *"The unexamined life is not worth living"* (Socrates). Brian Tracy (2010: 32) also pointed out that: *"The happiest people in the world today are those who are living in harmony with their innermost convictions and values."*

Activity

There are psychometric instruments that trainers can use to help would-be entrepreneurs examine their values. For example, instruments related to work values, national culture and personality can be adapted in this exercise. A qualitative approach can also be used to help examine the trainees' values. The following question advanced by Brian Tracy (2010: 34) can be a basis for developing qualitative approaches to the examination of the trainees' values. These are questions such as:

- What is it that deep down in your heart, more than anything else, you would like to be, have or do in life?

- What words would you like people to use to describe you when you are not there?

- What would you like someone to say about you at your funeral?

- How would you want your family, friends, and children to remember you?

- What kind of reputation do you have today?

- What kind of reputation would you like to have sometime in the future?

- What would you have to begin doing today in order to create the kind of reputation that you desire?

These are fundamental questions right at the heart of the essence of life, and they provide an anchor to human endeavours. Therefore, trainees need to examine their past, present and future through the lens of their values.

5.2.4 Examination of Trainees' Beliefs

The natural progression from the determination of values is to the determination of the trainees' beliefs. Although values and beliefs go hand-in-hand, beliefs are more practical. They influence every decision from when to wake up and why, to what to eat, whether to talk to a stranger or not, etc. Beliefs are not necessarily the product of society, although they are influenced by it. Because of the pervasiveness and efficacy of beliefs in influencing daily behaviour, an individual belief system has a significant impact on entrepreneurial behaviour. To put it another way, successful entrepreneurs have a common belief system. For example research has found that successful entrepreneurs share the following characteristics which are borne out of their individual belief systems:

- Tenacious;
- Passionate;
- Visionary;
- Self-belief/confident;

- Flexible;
- Risk takers/thrill seekers;
- Creative destructors.

These are qualities that are anchored in an individual belief system. In other words, they are what it takes to be a successful entrepreneur.

It is important to help trainees to understand how their individual belief system can aid or constrain entrepreneurial ambition. There are well-established psychometric instruments that can be used to measure belief systems, but most significantly, entrepreneurial tendencies. Instruments that measure creativity, teamwork, learning styles, leadership and risk taking tendencies can be used to examine trainees' potential to be entrepreneurs. Also, more recent instruments that can examine spiritual and emotional intelligence can be used.

There are various sources of self-administered questionnaires online that trainees can be asked to use. For example, the following websites can help trainees to examine their tendencies and potential to run a business successfully.

- potentialentrepreneur.ac/client/Questionnaire
- www.bdc.ca/EN/advice_centre/benchmarking_tools/pages/entrep reneurial_self_assessment.
- www.psychometrictest.org.uk
- www.wrdf.org/wp-content/uploads/Entrepreneur_self_Assessment_surey.pdf
- www.mvp/cfee.org/en/selfassessisentforme.html

5.2.5 Setting Personal Goals

We argue throughout this book that the key to eradicating poverty should start by analysing the personal characteristics of the person, not just the situation he/she finds him/herself in. Most research and intervention on poverty reduction appears to focus almost exclusively on the circumstances of the poor, rather than digging deeper to explore whether individual characteristics play a part in the circumstances people find themselves in. Our discussion of the value and belief systems that guide behaviour in the previous sections is an attempt to highlight the relevance of individual characteristics in entrepreneurship training. Having determined the personal value and belief systems of trainees, an entrepreneurship training programme should focus attention on how to develop personal goals. As the saying goes, "People who do not have a goal in life; they do not need to be told which path to take." In other words, the essence of entrepreneurial training for poverty reduction should not be about how to set up and run a successful business. It should be about how the business can achieve personal goals. As Stephen Covey says, "Always begin with the end in mind."

5.2.6 Personal Goals

When training for poverty reduction, trainees should be sensitised about the importance of personal goals. Goals can be and should be a major motivator to drive people out of poverty. Therefore, the training programme should help trainees to establish their personal goals. Within the themes of spirituality, system thinking, and interdependence, personal goals should be within the context of the individual and the long-term advancement of the community. To be more specific, personal goals should relate to the following question: "What would you like people to say about you when you are no longer around?" We argue that when there is a sufficient critical mass of people whose personal goals relate to the question above, and they successfully achieve the goals, there will be a significant reduction in poverty in Africa. Therefore, the training of entrepreneurs for poverty reduction in Africa should make the setting of personal goals a priority.

Activity

There are several exercises that help trainees develop their personal goals. It is likely they will confuse goals with objectives. Trainers should help them distinguish the two. The former are long-term in nature and can be less quantifiable than objectives.

An objective could be the starting and registering of their business, while the goal could be achieving financial independence or getting out of poverty. Another objective could be hiring 5 employees from within the community, while a related goal could be to contribute to reducing the unemployment of young people. The characteristics of the objectives and goals should be clarity and specificity, and be achievable and measurable.

Trainees can be asked to write a list of things they want to achieve by setting up their businesses. This will provide an idea of their goals. Then, a similar question should be asked, which is what they hope to achieve within a certain timeline e.g. one month, six months, one year to five years. This will give an idea of their objectives. The trainer can then help them categorize them in terms of goals and objectives, as well as their characteristics in terms of clarity, how specific they are, etc.

In setting their goals, the trainees should be guided by seven keys to personal goals (Tracy, 2010: 64). The seven keys are: (1) clarity, specificity, detail, and written down; (2) measurable and rational; (3) time bound; (4) challenging; (5) harmonious and congruent with values and beliefs; (6) balanced with work and life; (7) a definite purpose for life. The seven keys to personal goals should help the trainees to develop clear and achievable goals. When the developed personal goals have been achieved, they should contribute to poverty reduction within the community. Our point of departure here is that if poverty reduction is to succeed through entrepreneurship in Africa, then personal goals should be intertwined with social or communal goals. The pursuit of highly individualized and hard-nosed personal economic goals as preached by the current interventions in poverty reduction is inadequate in addressing poverty in Africa, hence, our advocacy throughout this book of "spirituality," system thinking, and interdependence. The following section provides practical steps for setting and achieving personal goals. These should be the foundation for setting and achieving business goals. The weakness of entrepreneurship training in Africa is that more often than not, trainees are taught how to set and achieve business goals, neglecting the fact that business goals cannot be sustainably achieved if personal goals are not considered. Therefore, we advocate the use of personal goals as a foundation for building business goals.

5.2.7 Practical Steps in Developing Personal Goals as a Foundation for Building Business Goals

Desire: It is not enough to have a goal no matter how worthy, without the desire to achieve it. Desire provides the energy required to pursue a worthy goal. In his classic book, "Think and Grow Rich," Napoleon Hill identified a burning desire as the main ingredient for success in whatever goal a person is pursuing. The half-hearted pursuit of a goal does not deliver anything but frustration. Trainees who just jump on the bandwagon of starting up a business without a burning desire to succeed in the endeavour would be better off considering other careers. Trainers should help the trainees to identify their burning desire. As we have seen in the previous chapters, SMEs in Africa face unique challenges. The enormity of the challenges will double if the SME operator has no burning desire to succeed. One of the main challenges for any intervention to address unemployment and poverty reduction is the issue of identifying those who have a burning desire to succeed, as opposed to those who have a burning need to survive. In the land of the needy, it is easy to confuse the two.

Those who have a burning need to get out of poverty are not necessarily the people who have a burning desire to succeed in business.

The challenge is for the trainers to impress on the trainees that their need to set up a business is not the same as a burning desire. One way to identify the burning desire of trainees is to examine the sacrifices they have made in pursuit of their dreams. One-to-one discussions exploring the life histories of trainees can help them reveal their burning desires, if they have them. If they do not have any burning desires, all is not lost, because some people might not be aware that a burning desire is the key to success. This is because childhood experiences and socialization could have given them the impression that success comes from prayers in mosques or churches, or from going on pilgrimages to certain sacred sights, rather than from developing a burning desire and working hard to achieve it. In African society where belief systems emphasize the role of the supernatural in determining one's destiny, the concept of a burning desire is not always recognised as a key ingredient for success. Therefore, entrepreneurship training should focus on changing the mindsets of trainees and orienting them towards developing the burning desire for their goals.

Believe in your goal: An important step in practicalizing the goal set by the would-be entrepreneur is having the belief and confidence that the goal is achievable. This is based on the assumption that the goal is achievable in the first place. It is the role of the trainers to help trainees develop the goals that are achievable rather than *pie in the sky*. Belief in the achievement of the goals provides the person with the energy to continue following the path that will lead to success. Trainees must believe that there is light at the end of the tunnel. The social and economic situation in Africa has developed a mindset amongst many people which underpins feelings of despair and hopelessness. Business operators cannot succeed when they harbour this mindset. The training program must try to debunk this idea of hopelessness and encourage trainees to develop a mindset of optimism and hope for good things to come in the very near future. Trainees must believe in their heart of hearts that their situation will change. They should be counselled to believe that it is possible to get out of poverty through entrepreneurial spirit. They should be given home-grown examples of people who have escaped poverty through developing successful businesses. Visiting speakers from "rags to riches" should be invited to speak to trainees and provide them with life stories of inspiration and optimism.

Goals should be written down: Trainees must write down their goals and memorise them to be reminded what their endeavour is about. It is very easy to lose sight of what the business is about. It is very easy to lose sight of why they are undergoing the training. The idea of writing down a goal comes from simple logic that says, "Whatever you do, you will remember it. Whatever you hear or think, you are likely to forget it." By writing down your goal, you are using multiple senses in the process. The more senses you use, such as hearing, feeling, and seeing, the more likely you will understand and remember. Most importantly, experts argued that when you write down your goal and place it where you can see it frequently, it will help you keep focus and guide your thinking and daily activities. Therefore, trainees should be asked to write down their goals in a simple, understandable and "catchy" way so that it helps them measure their journey and assess their daily behaviour against the goals they wish to achieve. Trainees should be able to state their goals in a few words and at the drop of a hat.

Trainees should be provided with examples of written goals that can set an example of how personal goals should be written. We encourage trainers to use local examples, not examples delivered from America or Europe. Goals from America or Europe are not likely to develop the strong belief that such goals are achievable because the environment where such extraordinary achievements took place does not exist in Africa. Therefore, some people are not likely to be inspired by the use of such achievements as examples of what is possible. The use of home-grown success stories is more likely to inspire people. Trainers should prepare home-grown success stories to be used in the entrepreneurship training. These cases should demonstrate that despite the harsh economic and social environment, many people are able to realise their dreams of setting up and running successful SMEs.

Baseline Determination: An important action for putting personal goals into practice is the assessment of personal qualities and the capacity to achieve the goal. The assessment of the baseline should be as honest as possible. It should not only be confined to what the trainee can do, but also what and how the personal circumstances of the person can enable or constrain the achievement of the goal. In an African context, personal circumstances can include the immediate family, the extended family, friends, and the culture and tradition. There is a diversity of traditions in Africa which can constrain or enable entrepreneurship. Some societies have a strong entrepreneurial tradition while others are weaker. For example, the people of the Igbo tribe of South Eastern Nigeria are renowned for their entrepreneurial and enterprising spirit. Therefore, it is easier for a trainee from such a community to benefit from the support and experience of such a community which is already familiar with the challenges and opportunities associated with setting up and running an SME.

In a nutshell, assessing the baseline should include assessing personal experience, education, interests, the impact of family and friends, and tribal traditions. We suggest the following template should be used by trainers to help trainees establish their baseline. The baseline should help the trainees determine their own starting point in the journey to achieve their goal. Most importantly, the assessment of the personal situation should help the trainees determine the goals that are achievable. As Tracy (2010: 69) pointed out:

> When you assess your situation by analysing your starting point, you are forced to be honest with yourself. This enables you to set goals that are believable and achievable rather than setting goals that may be unattainable and self-defeating.

Table 5.2: Assessing Your Baseline

Quality and Capacity	Positives	Negatives
Experience		
Education		
Personality		
Financial Capital		

Assess your social capital: Social scientists and especially economists, have argued that people can derive social and economic benefit by being part of a group; the wider the network the more the social and economic benefits. In fact, this idea is not new to African society. This is why Africans have developed an extended family system rather than a nucleolus family system. The harsh environment ensures that this notion of an extended family system still persists. However, some people have more effective networks than others. Before setting up the business, it is vital that the would-be entrepreneur assesses his/her social capital. They should also assess the effectiveness of their social networks. It is not a bad idea to make a list of the people, associations and organizations with which the entrepreneur is intimately familiar. In an African context, social capital can enable and constrain an entrepreneur. On the plus side, the entrepreneur can use social capital to access business opportunities and negotiate favourably with clients. Social capital can enable the entrepreneur to build a customer base because of the emotional attachment with the customers. In other words, the entrepreneur can leverage the social capital to expand his/her market, and to access labour and support from institutions and organizations. Trainers should emphasize the need for assessing social capital and determine if the trainees appreciate that their social capital can make or break their ambition in running a successful business. They should appreciate that setting up a business in certain sectors or industries is harder without social capital. In fact, on the negative side of the argument, social capital has been used successfully to fend off entry to a specific area of business. Therefore, trainees should determine if they have the adequate social capital to pursue their goal in a specific industry. They should consider if they should change their goal to match the assessment of their social capital. Trainees should be asked to make a list of the members of their networks and explain what and how they can contribute to their goal. It should be pointed out that social networks can be a source of burden to the business in an African context. The network of friends and family can use the business as a source of social security, which if the entrepreneur is not careful, can be the catalyst for the destruction of the business.

Table 5.3: Assessing Social Capital

Network	Positives	Negatives	What They Can contribute	How They Can Contribute
Family				
Friends				
Classmates				
Extended Family				
Associations				
Public Institutions				

Assessing your reputation: in some societies, the personal knowledge of the business operator is a key determinant of business success. Therefore starting a business in such societies will require taking stock of one's reputation in the community. The reputation of family members and even a tribal or clan affiliation can enable or constrain the success of the business. There are stereotypes in every society. Some people or tribes may be viewed as more trustworthy in business than others. Trust is an indispensable commodity in running a business. It is the foundation for running a successful business. It is better not to have any reputation than have a bad reputation. This is because it is easier to build a reputation than to repair a reputation. Trainees should be asked to take an honest and serious assessment of their reputation before they set their goals. They should ask questions such as, what am I known for? Does my family have a particular reputation in the community? Does my tribe or clan have a reputation in relation to running a business in the industry/sector I want to operate in? How do these reputations affect my goal? The answer to these questions should help the trainee set a realistic and achievable goal.

Need and Want Determination: An important element in setting a personal goal is the determination of what the goal is supposed to achieve. It is not enough to set a goal. Trainees need to be clear in their minds of the ultimate purpose of achieving the goal. Clear determination of needs and wants should help establish the purpose of the goal. In other words, needs and wants are the reasons why the goal is set. The reasons should be the fuel that drives the pursuit of the goal. We should emphasize that these reasons should be worthy reasons. They should be related to the theme of spirituality, system thinking, and interdependence. It is counter intuitive that interdependent or communal needs and wants are more likely to lead to the achievement of personal wants and needs. Trainers should ask the trainees to list the reasons why they set the goals they have set for themselves. The list should be analysed and discussed within the context of spirituality, system thinking, and interdependence. A trainee might set a goal of financial independence. He/she should be asked to give a reason why he/she wants to be financially independent.

Timeline: One of the most important elements in goal setting is the establishment of a deadline for the goal to be achieved. We stated earlier that objectives are short-term aims or goals. To achieve the main personal goal, the short-term objectives must be achieved. Setting a deadline for each objective and the main personal goal can act as a motivator, a point of reference, and a measure of progress. Experts argue that much more can be achieved when goals are broken down into daily activities, as opposed to just chasing the goal without measuring progress using a timeline. In fact, the entrepreneur is unlikely to gain the support of some benefactors if he/she is unable to indicate his/her goal and when he/she hopes to achieve it. Setting a timeline can boost confidence in the entrepreneur, as well as generate confidence in people and institutions that are willing to help the entrepreneur. Therefore, a key activity in the training programme is to ask the trainees to set deadlines for the achievement of the short-term objectives and the personal goal.

Setting a deadline is not an exact science. However, trainees should make an educated guess, taking into account their strengths and weaknesses, as well as the business and social environment. The deadline for the goal should be discussed and analyzed within the context of a SWOT analysis of the person. Based on the analysis and discussion, obstacles to the achievement of the goal can be identified. This might lead to specific interventions such as acquiring more knowledge and skills, building social capital, building a reputation, counselling, mentoring, etc.

Developing a Personal Plan: Setting a personal goal is not a guarantee for achieving the goal even if all the resources required to achieve the goal are available. There must be a plan for the execution of the goal. A list of activities has to be identified and prioritised. Resources have to be identified and prioritised. Both financial and non-financial costs need to be identified. A timeline needs to be set for each activity. There should be a performance management system regardless of how informal or rudimentary the system is. It should help measure progress in the achievement of personal goals. The following template can be used to develop a plan for the achievement of a personal goal.

Table 5.4: Plan for Personal Goal

	Activities	Target	Measures	Resources	Initiatives	Timeline
1						
2						
3						
4						
5						
6						

5.2.8 What happens next?

Having developed a plan for achieving a personal goal, the major task of achieving the goal will start. The main challenge is changing oneself. As the saying goes, to change your condition, you must first change yourself. Poverty cannot be changed without changing the internal condition that created the poverty in the first place. For many, if not most people, their condition is created by their own thinking and behaviour rather than by the external environment. The proof of this statement can be demonstrated by the success of people who are in an identical situation but manage to get out of it, while others in an identical situation languish in poverty. What then are the steps for getting out of poverty? The following are some of the steps to be taken to make a change in a personal life that can lead to the eradication of poverty.

Change your thinking: Trainers should underscore the need for entrepreneurs to change their thinking from a negative and hopeless mindset to a positive and optimistic state. Let the trainees understand that they have a choice to either think negatively or positively regardless of their circumstances. Positive thinking does not mean to surrender to poverty or tolerate and deny the challenges. It means to recognise the challenges and accept that life is not a bed of roses. However, people must be prepared to take advantage of the challenges and use them as an opportunity. The challenges can also be the basis of building character. Trainees should appreciate that every situation is changeable. No condition is permanent. Trainees should understand that their behaviour is the manifestation of their thinking. Their condition is the manifestation of their pattern of behaviour over time. It is easy in cultures where the external locus of control is dominant, to assume that their condition is always created by someone else. Or it is created by God. This way of thinking contradicts the logic of human existence. Most significantly, it contradicts Islamic and Christian teachings, where God encourages the followers of the religions to pray and ask for his guidance and support. This basically means that followers must do something if they want their situation to change.

Discipline Yourself: Discipline is the most salient and important characteristic of successful people. Nothing can be achieved without discipline. Even unworthy goals cannot be achieved without discipline. Discipline is consistency in appropriate thoughts and behaviour. It is very challenging in African society to develop and establish entrepreneurial discipline. This is because in a highly social and extended family system, it is not easy to demarcate business from non-business time and resources. Yet, if the discipline is not developed, then the business has no chance of succeeding. This is why we advocate that an entrepreneurship training program should not be confined to the entrepreneur alone. Members of the family and immediate community should be sensitised on the need to support the entrepreneur by offering moral support through allowing him/her to put into practice what he/she has learned. They should understand and appreciate that the success of the entrepreneur will be their own success. Conversely, the failure of the business is their own failure. This is because the model of the business is built on poverty reduction and societal achievement.

Change your habits: Here we are referring to behavioural habits, not thinking habits. There are certain habits that are incompatible with running a successful business. Some of these habits are borne out of culture and tradition. For example, some people can develop lousy time management habits very early in life. The habits might be incompatible with running a successful business. Similarly, people can develop habits such as flamboyance or excessive generosity which are not compatible with running a successful business, or the spirituality and system thinking advocated in this book. African culture and traditions in certain societies encourage flamboyance and excessive generosity. Although the business model advocated in this book encourages entrepreneurs to exhibit virtuous behaviour such as generosity, this should not be to the detriment of the business. This is because one cannot help the poor by being poor oneself. The easiest way to change a habit is not by stopping the habit but by replacing it. Rather than saying, "I will stop socializing with people because it is wasting precious time for business," say "I will use my time to develop my business." Rather than saying, "This month I will not accept any invitations for weddings," say, "I will devote the whole of this month to developing my business plan and establishing contacts with clients." Training programs should help entrepreneurs identify the habits that are incompatible with business success and provide them with an effective means of eradicating these habits.

Seven Habits of Highly Effective People: In this section, we summarise the classic book of Stephen Covey in which he advocated 'seven habits that characterise highly effective people. The first habit is to always be proactive with the understanding that the decisions you make about anything will determine your effectiveness and your ultimate condition in the long-term. Even not making a decision is by itself a decision. Therefore, it is better to be proactive than to allow your circumstances to determine your faith. Successful business people live by this motto. The second habit advocated by Stephen Covey states that you should always behave with the end in mind. Having identified your values and beliefs which set the foundation of your personal goal, your future actions should be compatible with your personal goals. The third habit states that you should put first things first. That means your daily activities within and outside the business should be geared towards achieving the end. The choices you make should be guided by the end state you aspire to. The fourth habit to develop is a win-win habit. This is what we have advocated throughout this book within the theme of system thinking and spirituality. The fifth habit to develop that can lead to effectiveness is to seek first to understand before you expect to be understood. This requires the development of the habit of empathy. In other words, before you expect sympathy from people, you need to empathise with them. You need to understand their point of view. Be in their shoes for a few seconds.

The sixth habit that will lead to effectiveness is developing a synergy among people. Any successful person relies on others for input, either in ideas or other resources. This is what Napoleon Hill calls mastermind. You need to develop a team of people you can trust who can provide you with a diversity of input. You need to select people based on merit, not based on emotional attachment. Successful business people in Africa do not always rely on their family for mastermind unless they can prove they merit it. Unsuccessful people more often than not tend to go for "cheap inputs" from family and friends who have no clue on how to run a business. The cheapest commodity in the African community is advice. Everyone you are on talking terms with can offer advice–from personal to business. Trainees need to be sensitive about the need to pick their mastermind carefully. The seventh habit is what Stephen Covey calls "sharpen the saw." This refers to balancing and renewing your resources, energy, and your health to achieve a sustainable lifestyle. You need to have a balanced life style in order for the business to be successful. Besides, the business is not an end, but a means to an end.

5.3 Conclusion

Central to this chapter is the argument that the success of an SME will depend on the quality of the person operating the enterprise. By implication, the success of the poverty reduction intervention which focuses on training the unemployed will depend on the quality of the trainees themselves. The program cannot eradicate poverty if the targeted people have not got what it takes to run a successful business. This is why the chapter advocates the need to focus training interventions on the trainee's personal characteristics rather than to train them on running a successful business. This should be the starting point for every training intervention using business as a route to get out of unemployment and poverty. The chapter has underscored the importance of assessing their own beliefs and values, and they can help or constrain the running of a successful business. A significant portion of the chapter is devoted to setting personal goals that are in line with spirituality, system thinking and interdependence. We conclude the chapter by advocating the application of the seven habits of highly effective people. To sum up, this chapter is particularly targeted at trainers as much as trainees undergoing entrepreneurship training.

CHAPTER SIX

STRATEGIC MANAGEMENT OF SMEs
FROM THE POVERTY REDUCTION PERSPECTIVE

6.1 Introduction

In the preceding chapters we have outlined and discussed the context and backgrounds within which SMEs operate on the African continent. We also laid the foundation upon which SMEs can be managed to ensure that the goal of poverty reduction is attained through the spiritual approach to policy formulation, implementation and SME management. This chapter addresses how SMEs should operate if they are to contribute to sustainable poverty reduction through job creation. The discipline of Strategic Management is used here to provide an understanding and techniques for managing a successful SME. The approach adopted in this chapter is unconventional in the sense that the theme of *Spirituality* will be deployed as the lens through which Strategic Management is viewed and discussed. The chapter starts by discussing and defining the purpose of an SME as a business, followed by how an SME can achieve its purpose through strategic management processes. The issue of SME competitiveness is discussed throughout the chapter within the contexts of poverty reduction, the African business environment, spirituality and system thinking. The chapter concludes by advocating the need to consider the collaborative rather than the competitive approach to running SMEs in Africa.

6.2 Setting the Vision and Mission for the SME
in the Poverty Reduction Context

6.2.1 The need for a Vision for the SME

Every SME should operate guided by a vision rather than by a day-to-day reaction to the environment, short-term objectives or goals. In other words, SME operators must have a vision for the business; otherwise the sustainability of the business will be called into question. It is important that SME operators and prospective entrepreneurs do not confuse their own vision with the vision for the business. While the mission concerns what the SME is delivering to the customer and society, the vision should be about the *dream* pertaining to how the business can be even more successful in its mission. A vision is a very long-term goal rather than a five- or ten-year objective. A vision should be a state of being for the business rather than a measurable target. For example, a vision for the SME could be "graduating into a large-scale enterprise". Or it could be to become "one of the most respected businesses in the community", or the most "socially responsible" business in the community, or "to eradicate poverty" in the community, to be "financially independent" or to be "the most preferred brand". Other types of visions might relate to innovation, society, the customer or the world at large. For an African SME of course, has to have a down-to-earth localised dream in the beginning. Later it can revisit its vision. A vision is not plucked out of the air. It should be based on the sound core values of the SME operators. Within the context of poverty reduction, a societal imperative that has economic consequences to the business should be reflected in the vision of the SME. The vision should be translated into the mission of the SME. Visions are not always explained in absolute monetary terms. Yet they provide many advantages in terms of inspiration, guidance, motivation and decision making which should lead to economic and societal benefits.

6.2.2 The Imperative of the Mission (Purpose) of the SME

Purpose: Before starting on the concept of *SMEs' Missions*, we felt readers need to be reminded of the notion of *purpose* which, ironically, is supposed to be synonymous with mission. However, *Purpose* has taken a back seat lately. Purpose has a deeper meaning than mission. What is a *Purpose?* A purpose is the essence of why a person, a position or job, an enterprise, an institution or a nation, exists. Therefore, a *Purpose* is more than what a person does, what people do, what a company manufactures, or what a leader does. Purpose is perhaps encapsulated in the following quotations:

> Just about everything that has happened in my life since I made that teenage resolution has proved to me that Purpose is crucial for all truly successful enterprises. Let others play with 'strategy' and 'tactics' and 'management'. Purpose is the game of champions. Only strong-minded men and women–adults with powerful intellects and real character and spine of steel–are suited for it. (Mourkogiannis, 2006: 5)

> There are some fundamental beliefs you have to share with a group of people. And if you don't have those fundamental beliefs, then the rest of the stuff–the little things–have nothing to hang on to, so they don't become as meaningful to implement on an individual basis. (Pfeffer & Sutton, 1999; *cited in Mourkogiannis*, 2006: 123)

The reader might have noticed that the last statement is talking about spirituality which was discussed in the previous chapter. The statement was made by a manager referring to how a company can achieve its objectives through people. The company is a highly successful company by world standards. It shows not only that people seek to do something meaningful to reflect their essence in life, but that even companies are expected to exist for something more meaningful than just making money for the shareholders. In a nutshell, the discussion and quotations underscore the importance or even the necessity of centralizing and instilling the notion of purpose in the minds of African entrepreneurs and SME operators. Every SME should have its purpose (e.g. poverty eradication) articulated and engraved in the minds of those operating within it. This will be a key determinant of the success of the SME sector as a vehicle for poverty eradication. As we will advocate later, SMEs and prospective entrepreneurs would need to collaborate, rather than focus exclusively on competition. Collaboration within the African context will be hard, if not impossible, without a greater sense of purpose. In other words, the absence of a greater sense of purpose is partly responsible for why most people entering into business in Africa tend to *go it alone*. Even when there is collaboration amongst SME owner operators, it is usually on a shorter term basis or in minor inconsequential areas such as sharing transportation equipment or premises. The following provides ten steps that can help SMEs to develop a purpose for the business:

1.   Review Strategy;
2.   Draw out implications;
3.   Understand your moral ideas;
4.   Understand the business' traditions (if it has any);
5.   Take a purpose inventory;
6.   Take a moral inventory of the community;
7.   Identify a purpose;
8.   Create a metrics and models;
9.   Test strategy and purpose;
10.   Decide and launch a campaign to make the purpose work. (Mourkogiannis, 2006: 180)

Mission: The notion of mission is the starting point for any discussion about organizational effectiveness and success. This is because any judgement about an organizational success that is not linked to its mission is a waste of time and energy. What then should be the mission of an organization against which to judge its success? The *mission* of any organization, whether it is a private or public/NGO entity, is to serve particular stakeholder(s). In other words, it is the reason why the organization exits. Therefore, to be a viable and long-term business concern, the SME has to continue to serve its stakeholders. However, the starting point in serving the stakeholders is understanding who the stakeholders are and what they need and want. Another important element of a mission is the understanding of the type of business the SME is engaged in. Within the context of poverty reduction, SME operators need to clarify in their minds that their key stakeholders are not only the customers, but also the communities to which they belong. However, a critical question many people might ask is: why would a business operator takes his/her eyes *off the ball* and start focusing on the community? Within the African and poverty reduction contexts, the *health* of the community is as important as the *health* of the business. It is essential that the idea of the *community imperative* is impressed on SME operators. They should appreciate that the business will only survive if the society survives. The business will only survive if there is social stability and security for example. Most importantly, they should appreciate that African countries have weak institutions. Therefore, they have to step in and fill the gaps left by state institutions. Otherwise their businesses will not survive in the long run. Unlike developed countries where businesses rely on institutions for maintaining law and order as well as for providing safety nets, SMEs in Africa should not expect national institutions to provide such services to the community; neither do they provide them effectively anyway. Therefore, SMEs should incorporate, as part of their mission, the creation of jobs in the community which serves as a means of addressing the potential social ills that can affect the business in the long run. This is what *Spirituality in Business* is advocating in this book. That is, doing "good" for the community is "good business". We are not talking about *social responsibility* here. We are talking about the *social imperative* of a business. Nor should this mission be confused with social entrepreneurism. This is because the main focus of social entrepreneurism is to run a business for the benefit of the community or society. In fact, a social entrepreneurial concern might not even have job creation as part of its mission. This is because it is the proceeds of the business operation that are used to support the community. This mission has to be deliberate and conscious rather than seen as a by-product of running a business.

6.2.3 What should be included in the Mission of SMEs for Poverty Reduction?

The SME must have a precise and concise mission statement that is meaningful to the operator as well as to those operating within it. Without a precise mission statement based on the understanding of spirituality and poverty reduction, the SMEs might not only struggle to achieve the goal of poverty reduction, but also fail to achieve sustainability. In a nutshell, a mission statement for the SME provides a sense of direction for the business, the operator and the employees. It also helps the state and international development agencies to have a clear understanding of what the business is engaged in and how they can help it. A good mission statement can therefore enable the SME to have access to public goods nationally and internationally. This is because many donors and development agencies have wised up to the fact that, to help the poor, they need to identify effective organizations who can deliver. A mark of effectiveness is the clear demonstration of knowing what business the SME is engaged in.

It is worth pointing out that a good mission statement need not be elaborate and lengthy. Experts argue that a shorter mission statement is better. This is because it is easier to communicate the mission to the stakeholders. The mission statement that can provide stakeholders with the sense of direction and enable development agencies to target their support effectively is:

1.   The mission statement should have a clear statement of *purpose*, what goods and/or services the SME delivers, and for whom. SME operators need to be able to articulate the generic goods or services they deliver. They should be able to define their customers as well as key stakeholders. Most effective mission statements include the goods and services that are produced, the categories of customers, and how the goods and services are produced. The question regarding the production of goods and services leads to the question: who produces them; i.e. the employees. Within the context of poverty reduction, the mission statement should include an indication of how employees are valued: in other words, the philosophy of managing people.

2.   The mission statement should clearly articulate the principles and beliefs that guide the business. These are widely referred to as *values*. This is the point where the concept of *spirituality* comes in. For entrepreneurial training purpose, we strongly advocate trainers to be trained in how to help SME operators to articulate the values of a sustainable business. The concept of *spirituality in business* will provide the foundation for achieving this objective. In the previous chapter we have highlighted the key aspects of spiritual traits and how they can be used in the training and development of SME operators. The traits can be used during strategic planning training for SME operators and prospective entrepreneurs.

Implications for the Training and Development of SME Operators and Entrepreneurs

This book intends to provide practitioners with practical ideas on developing would-be entrepreneurs and SME operators. The preceding discussion has implications for training and developing people in the SME sector. Interventions regarding poverty reduction through business start-ups should start with the idea of a vision and mission, rather than technical skills such as business planning, market survey and record keeping. Trainees should be sensitised in the notion of the "purpose of a business" as well as the "motive behind starting a business". Note, the two are not the same. In the poverty reduction context there should be a strong alignment between the two. For example, in a normal context, the purpose of the entrepreneur setting up a business is exclusively to make money for him/herself, although in the process, as a by-product, the business will serve the community. In a poverty reduction context on the other hand, trainers should impress on the trainees very early on that, for the business to be sustainable in the long run, it has to have a dual purpose: to serve the customer and serve the community. This means serving the customer through the provision of goods or services, and serving the community through job creation.

Trainees should be put through a series of exercises demonstrating the business case for the need to have a dual purpose for the business in the poverty reduction context. The concepts of spirituality and system thinking can help in establishing the economic benefits of linking the business and the community.

The other dimension of purpose is the individual purpose. Trainees should be helped to identify a greater meaning from the business rather than solely material gain. Again, the concept of spirituality can help to achieve this goal. Would-be entrepreneurs and SME operators should be helped to identity meaning from this endeavour. They should be helped to understand how to acquire pleasure from helping the community rather than from material acquisition through the business. Even where material acquisition is pursued, it is because it will help the community. For example, the SME operator might try to expand the business premises because it will create jobs for the builders,

furniture makers and artisans in the community. Different scenarios can be integrated in the training programme to deliberately demonstrate how SME operators can make conscious decisions that will benefit the community without burdening the business at all.

6.2.4 Setting the Long-term and Short-term Objectives for the SME

Talk to any successful person in any area of endeavour and they will affirm that they could not achieve success without ambition. Ambition is articulated in the form of long-term (*Goals*) and short-term objectives. Objectives are the starting point for developing a strategy. In other words, *the choice of path to follow depends on where one wants to go.* Apart from helping to choose strategies, objectives provide a means of evaluating performance across the business (e.g. employees and units or departments). Within the context of poverty reduction, objectives can help evaluate how effective the business has been in reducing poverty by counting the number of people employed in the business against set targets.

Long-term objectives (i.e. Goals) are supposed to be broad and less specific, but clear enough to provide a sense of direction to guide the behaviour of managers regarding the focus on the long-term perspectives. For example, a long-term objective is to break even; while the short-term objective is to reduce the cost of transportation by 5% in the next six months. Another example of a goal is achieving market leadership, while the short-term objective is increasing sales by 3% annually. Table 6-1 provides a template on how to set short-term and long-term objectives.

Table 6-1. Template for Setting Short-term and Long-term Objectives

Key Areas for Objectives	Short-term Objectives	Long-term Objectives
Financial 1. 2. 3. 4.	——— ——— ———	——— ——— ———
Production/Operation 1. 2. 3. 4.	——— ——— ———	——— ——— ———

Human Resource 1. 2. 3. 4.	—————— —————— ——————	—————— —————— ——————
Technology 1. 2. 3. 4.	—————— —————— ——————	—————— —————— ——————
Marketing 1. 2. 3. 4.	—————— —————— ——————	—————— —————— ——————
Customer Service 1. 2. 3. 4.	—————— —————— ——————	—————— —————— ——————
Job creation 1. 2. 3. 4.	—————— —————— ——————	—————— —————— ——————
Societal Image 1. 2. 3. 4.	—————— —————— ——————	—————— —————— ——————

The template above provides broad areas where short-term and long-term objectives can be set. The SME should break down those areas in more detail to identify more specifically the current situation regarding the key areas, which long- and short-term objectives should be set, and where they should be set. Regardless of the area, each must meet certain criteria otherwise it will not serve the purpose of guidance and measurement, for example. First, the objective must be stated in a precise and specific fashion. In other words, the objective should be quantifiable, so that when it is achieved everybody will know it has been achieved. Second, the objective must be measurable especially by the person who is to achieve it.

It is not enough to provide a quantifiable objective, there must be a system and a tool to measure the achievement. Third, the objective must be realistic and challenging. This means that it should act as a motivator. Fourth, there must be a timeframe against which the achievement can be measured.

6.3 Developing a Competitive Edge for the SME as a Business

Having developed a mission statement, the next important step is to decide how to develop a competitive edge. This is due to that fact that although the SME might have a social imperative in its mission, it has to act like a true business entity. Whatever it produces, there will be other businesses that produce the same or similar products. Therefore, the SME should think how it can set itself apart from other businesses. In order to come up with the way to differentiate itself the SME should ask and answer the following question: *why would customers patronise us rather than other businesses that compete with us?* This means that the SME has to think of the ways it can excel. This can be through one of the business processes or the product or service, or several combinations. It can use the concept of the value chain (Porter, 1985) to identify a combination of activities that will make the SME stand out and establish a unique image in the minds of customers and stakeholders. The competitive edge it develops must be sustainable. For it to be sustainable it should not be easy to copy, and it must continue to create value for the customer. We believe the social imperative to be adopted by the SME in making poverty reduction as part of its mission will be a powerful tool that contributes to its competitive advantage. The community will appreciate the contribution that the SME is making by employing members of the community. This should give the business an advantage over businesses that are in the community just to make money. The following section elaborates more fully how the SME can develop a competitive advantage.

6.3.1 Ways to Develop a Competitive Edge

Core Values: Any business that wants to be successful in the long-term should develop core values that will guide the behaviour of its members. Ironically, such values do not only serve the business in terms of guiding the behaviour of its members, but help customers make decisions on whether they should deal with the company. Developing appropriate values that will guide the business decisions and daily actions of its members can be a significant competitive advantage. The SME should be known for a particular value system that is in tune with the community within which it operates. Again, the idea of doing business that will help poverty reduction can be a foundation on which the SME will build its core values. Through this, the people will see the business as part of the fabric of the community which needs to be supported through patronage since the beneficiaries of the going concern include members of the community. From the point of view of training and developing SME operators and prospective entrepreneurs, they should be helped to develop core values that will appeal to the community.

Product: We have seen in the previous section that part of the mission statement is the identification of the product delivered to the customer. In order to develop a competitive advantage, an SME needs to determine how it might differentiate its product from competitors' products. In other words, what value does the product offer to customers that the competitors' products do not offer? This is where creativity and innovation will be required. Since most SMEs in Africa do not create, manufacture and deliver their own products; except those in the service sector; the only means of differentiating their products is through other activities in the value chain. A packing and delivery system can be a means to building a competitive edge by the SMEs. The other means is by sourcing supplies from reputable vendors whose products are known to have quality and integrity. Even stocking products that are always in demand within the community can help build a competitive advantage.

Customer Service: Another important way to differentiate an SME from other SMEs operating in the same market is through providing a unique service which others do not or cannot provide. This requires constant innovation and creativity. The service can be at the point of sale or after sale. Formal or informal customer surveys can be a great way to identify what customers feel and want from the service offered during the transaction. Some customers might just want a smiling and courteous face. Others might want something more sophisticated and elaborate such as personalised service. The SME, regardless of its size and degree of formalization, should aspire to build a brand that distinguishes it from other SMEs. Unfortunately, even some large-scale enterprises sometimes do not take customer service seriously. They see it as a waste of money to dedicate time and resources after they have clinched the deal. Some give the impression that they are doing the customer a favour by selling the product to them. Customer service is a key to repeat business, and this is the most efficient way to ensure sales with limited marketing effort. From the point of view of poverty reduction, customer service offers an excellent opportunity to impress on the community that the business cares for them. Also, by being successful through customer service, the SME gets to stay in business and continue to employ members of the community.

Competitive Pricing: In Africa where the purchasing power of most people is low, an SME can differentiate itself from others by offering a competitive price for its goods and services. However, to achieve this goal the SME has to develop a strategy for doing so. For example, it has to develop a cost management strategy that will allow it to offer competitive pricing. Choosing the appropriate supplier or appropriate business model will allow the SME to offer a competitive price for the same product sold by its competitors. For example, Dell Computers was able to offer competitive prices for its computers by getting rid of the middle man. Apart from the benefits of supporting the community through affordable pricing, competitive pricing is a strong marketing tool in a society that is price-sensitive. It should be pointed out that competitive pricing does not mean that low quality products or services are sold cheaply. It means that a product that the customer values is sold at a lower price than the competitor.

Business Model and Business Process: These two concepts sometimes overlap in practice. On the one hand, a business model simply means the formula or blueprint that the SME uses to achieve its mission (i.e. serving the customer). A business process, on the other hand, is a collection and chain of activities with the end goal of serving the customer. In Michael Porter's value chain for example, there are lists of primary and support activities that form processes leading to the service of the customer. A business model or a particular business process can be a competitive advantage. An SME, no matter how small, can make a deliberate decision on how it can distinguish itself from others using a business model or using a particular business process. Customer service is a powerful process that can distinguish an SME from its competitors. For example, by simply hiring and motivating workers who are always courteous and helpful to the customers, the SME can have a competitive edge over its rivals. Developing trust" in the community and with customers can also be a business model which can make the business distinguishable from others. Trust was the only reason why the invention of commercial banking was a success, nothing more. In a nutshell, an SME should always strive to develop a formula for success. Developing a formula for success requires innovation, creativity and perseverance. Even a roadside mechanic can develop a business model or a business process that will have a competitive advantage.

6.4 Strategic Analysis for the SMEs

Having established a clear vision and a well-articulated mission, the SME needs to develop an overall strategy for delivering the mission and vision. This section presents a series of steps that the SME can take to develop such strategies. But first we need to explain what a strategy is from the point of view of managing an SME for poverty reduction in Africa. Strategy in this context is the *long-term oriented path* the SME follows or will follow, to deliver on its mission through a series of objectives including its vision. Given that no-one has the illusion that poverty will be eradicated overnight, the use of the phrase *long-term oriented path* is appropriate to describe an SME's strategy within the context of poverty reduction. It is perhaps important to bring in the issue of spirituality here, because following a long-term path requires a specific quality which is "spiritual" in nature. That quality is called *patience*. It is critical that when the *long-term oriented path* is developed, SME operators and their backers (e.g. policy makers and international donors) should exercise *patience* in following the *path*. This is because strategies take time to materialize. This is not to suggest that strategies should not be altered. In fact, one of the Strategy Gurus actually encouraged managers to alter their strategies when necessary (Mintzberg, 1998).

6.4.1 Examining the SME's Strengths and Weaknesses

The SME's pathway (strategy) to success must undergo serious analysis before it is laid down. It should start with a dispassionate and objective internal assessment. The SME should carry out an audit of its **Strengths**. This can start with assessing the qualities of the SME operator. Personality characteristics, as well as acquired qualifications, can be strengths that need to be assessed followed by a decision on how the qualities can be used to benefit the business. For example, the owner operator might be multilingual. This can be a major asset in the African context where there is a diversity of ethnicity in a community. Other aspects of internal strengths of the SME will include the quantity and quality of the employees, its public image, established loyal customers, innovative capacity, good business process and business model, etc. The main strength of the SME is regarded as its **core competency.** Every SME should try to develop a core competency. However, core competencies are not cast in stone. Core competencies can vary from one business to another and from time to time.

After assessing the strengths of the business, the next step is to assess its **weaknesses**. The weaknesses could emanate from similar areas identified as strengths, for example, an unskilled workforce, a poor public image, the poor personality of the owner or some key staff, etc. For a family run business, there could be a threat from the family members who might take advantage of the success of the business. Another potential problem could be siblings jockeying for position in the business. In a polygamous family there could be intense competition between siblings from different mothers. If not properly managed, the impact of polygamy as part of many African families could be a source of weakness in the business. It is worth pointing out that what might appear as a strength can turn out to be a weakness. Similarly, what seems like a weakness can turn out to be a strength.

By determining the **strengths** and **weaknesses** of the SME, the operator can get a full understanding of the business at a point in time. If it is a start-up, the prospective entrepreneur will have a sense of how the business will be from inception. As we indicated earlier, developing a strategy requires thorough analysis. An SME's strategy should be built on the foundation of its **strengths.** The strengths can be used against competitors' weaknesses or used to exploit opportunities. In the next chapter, we will discuss some of the management tools that SMEs can use during strategic planning. However, the table below provides a simple illustration of how such an assessment of strengths and weaknesses can be carried out by an SME.

Table 6-2. Template for Assessing the Strengths and Weaknesses of the SME

ANALYSIS OF STRENGTHS AND WEAKNESSES			COMMENTS
Potential	**Strength?**	**Weakness?**	
Physical Asset			
Financial Capital			
Cost structure			
Social Capital			
Public Image			
Personality, Skills and Experience of the Owner			
Personality, Skills and Experience of Staff			
Location			
Technology of Production			

Loyal Customer Base			
Potential to Scale Up			
Size			
Business Model			
Business Process			
Organization's Culture			

6.4.2 Examining the SME's Opportunities and Threats

Having assessed the internal environment of the business from the point of view of its strengths and weaknesses, SME must examine the external environment in terms of **Opportunities** and **Threats** to the survival and prosperity of the business. Opportunities are positive alternatives which the SME can take advantage of in order to achieve its mission, vision, and objectives within the context of poverty reduction. Although the African business environment for the SMEs might appear bleak, these are situations where real entrepreneurs come to the fore. With a bit of innovation, creativity and imagination, an SME operator can spot an opportunity and carve out a niche which can lead to success. The opportunities should be chosen based on the core competencies of the SME. There is no point pursuing an opportunity if the SME operator has not got the wherewithal to convert the opportunity into real benefits for the business. A spiritually endowed SME operator would resist falling into the trap of *chasing a wild goose* because he/she is devoid of mindless greed and is endowed with *patience*. There are many sources for opportunities that the SME can latch onto. However, these require imagination and tact. Nevertheless, the business environment offers various options for the SMEs. There are two ways to latch on to an opportunity. **First,** whether the particular phenomenon or incidence provides an opportunity to satisfy certain demand. **Second,** whether the particular phenomenon or incidence provides an opportunity to create demand. In both cases the SME needs to identify economic factors, demographic factors, technological factors, governmental initiatives and natural incidences that might lead to opportunities.

Threats to the existence and prosperity of SMEs abound, especially in the African context. SME operators need to constantly keep an eye on things that can threaten the existence or success of the business. At the strategic planning stage, an SME must familiarise itself with potential threats from the external environment. These would primarily include threats from the competition, the labour market, suppliers, government regulations, communal and societal unrest, the demographic and a health epidemic. The potential for these factors being threats to the business must be analysed. For a start-up business decision, the analysis of these factors and their potency could determine which business the entrepreneur gets into or when or how the business starts. For a small and vulnerable business, the choice of mode and time of entry is critical, otherwise the business will be "*dead on arrival*". If this happens, it will rob the entrepreneur and the community of the opportunity to contribute to poverty reduction through SMEs and job creation. Table 6-4 provides indicative broad sources of opportunities and threats relating to the business. Through brain storming, each factor can be broken down into minor details, leading to a clear identification of the potential impact of the factors.

Table 6-4. Template for Assessing the Opportunities for and Threats to the SME

Opportunities And Threats			COMMENTS
Potential	Opportunity?	Threat?	
Economic Factors			
Competition			
Demographic Factors			
Civil and Communal Instability			
Political Instability			
Technological Factors			
Supply Factors			
Governmental Initiatives			
Natural Incidences			
Health Epidemic			

6.4.3 Assessing the Competition

Although being a small business has its advantages, it comes with enormous challenges. One of the challenges is the ease of entry into the SME sector, particularly in an African context where institutional barriers are almost non-existent in most of the sectors, apart from the health sector. While the main advantage of ease of entry is the set-up cost, the disadvantage is competition. It means that the SME will not be operating on its own. Basically, it will be competing for customers, suppliers, and attention from key stakeholders. To most SME operators, especially those in the informal sector, the main challenge facing them is competition. Many do not realise the competition until it is too late. Therefore, as part of the strategic planning process, particular attention should be paid to assessing the level and nature of the competition (*Competitor Analysis*). For a start-up business, the essence of competitor analyses is encapsulated in the following statement *"before you enter the ring for a boxing match, you better know who you are up against"*.

When undertaking a *Competitor Analysis* it is vital that the competitors are categorised. This is because not all competitors have the same impact on the business. For example, a particular business can be categorised as a *direct competitor* because it recruits employees from the same labour market (i.e. hiring people with identical skills), and sells the same products or services. On the other hand, a business can be categorised as an *indirect competitor* if the business does not hire people with identical skills, but hires similar demographics in the same community with a high employment level. Also, a business can be classified as an *indirect competitor* if it sells a similar product but to a different market. How are competitor analyses carried out? In fact, how are all other analyses carried out? Within an African context, in all cases both formal and informal means would have to be used to collect the necessary information and data. We would encourage the constant collection of information and data through informal means as the business operates. The informal collection of data and information can be done through existing social networks. This is where the importance of building *social capital* comes to the fore. If an SME or its operator develops enough social capital, it will be easier to tap into the social capital to develop a database of information that is useful for making strategic decisions. Table 6-5 below provides guidelines on how to conduct competitive analyses.

Table 6-5. Template for Assessing the Competition

Key areas of Analyses	Conclusions drawn	Actions to be taken
Identity of direct competitors		
Identity of indirect competitors		
Specific area of the threat (e.g. Product, price, service etc)		
Location of the competitors		
Their strengths		
Their weaknesses		
Their business model compared to your own		
Their key strategy compared to your own		
Easy of entry into your industry		
Relationship with their customers		
Immediate and long term threat		
Potential for collaboration		

The information generated using **Table 6-5** above can be used to develop a specific strategy on how to deal with the competition. As we will be arguing later, one such approach is to "*collaborate with the enemy*". This is because sometimes collaboration is better than competition. The need to consider collaboration is in line with system thinking and spirituality discussed in the previous chapter. Also, the African business environment calls for a collaborative approach in order to develop an economy of scale that will ensure the profitability of some SMEs. This issue will be elaborated in the concluding part of this chapter.

6.5 Industry Analysis

Industry analysis is one of the important activities in the strategic planning process. The SME must understand the industry within which it operates. This is because the attractiveness of the industry will determine the profitability of the business (Porter, 1980). Thus, knowing the relative attractiveness of the types of industries that the SMEs are operating in can help to advise prospective entrepreneurs where to launch their start-up. SMEs in Africa do not entirely fit into one specific industry for obvious reasons; however, they do operate in a semblance of what can be categorised as industry. For example, those who decide to specialise in a particular product or a set of products or service(s) can be categorised into some kind of specific product or specific service industry. This allows for more sophisticated analyses of the categories of the SMEs' industries and for appropriate strategies to be pursued. For example, those who specialise in automobile repairs (roadside mechanics), the laundry business, business support services, personal grooming (e.g. barbers, hairdressing), painters and decorators, etc., can be categorised into specific industries where their characteristics can be analysed within the context of strategy.

Those in the grooming industry such as hairdressing and body make-up would have to be familiar with the profitability of the industry, the key challenges and reasons underlying the profitability, etc. Similarly, state and international development agencies must be familiar with the characteristics of the industries in which they are encouraging the youth and the unemployed to start their businesses. Otherwise, they will be leading a vulnerable group into a blind alley. The following sections describe how the competitiveness of SMEs can be analysed. Basically, their competitiveness can be analysed based on the bargaining power of Customers and Suppliers, the availability of substitutes for the SME's merchandise, the ease of entry into the SME's type of business and the rivalry amongst the SMEs (Porter, 1980). We would also like to add that within the African context at least, the willingness, ability and potential to collaborate can add to an SME's competitiveness.

6.5.1 Analysing the Bargaining Power of SMEs' Customers

It is crucial for the SME to determine the relative power of the customers of the business. An SME needs to know whether it is (in)dispensable to the customer and vice versa. Naturally, if the customer has an alternative source of supply, then the SME has to work very hard to keep the customer loyal. The SME should avoid blindly following the competitor's marketing strategies without knowing the power of the customer. The SME sector is highly competitive especially in the subsector (e.g. the informal sector) where there is ease of entry due to the low start-up capital required. Logically, the customers have more bargaining power when there are many competitors in a particular industry. Conversely, the customers will have less power if there are fewer competitors. The challenge for SMEs in Africa is the absence of data and information regarding the profile of competitors and customers. This is particularly challenging in the informal sector. Therefore, industry analysis in the SME sector is guesswork. However, an SME can do *educated guess work* if it has had long experience of operating in the sector. The data will be based on a patchwork of observation, gut-feeling, primary data, secondary information and rumours. Table 6-6 provides a template for analysing the industry within which the SME operates.

Table 6-6. Template for Analysing the Industry within which the SME Operates

Key Question	Yes	No	Implications for action
Can the SME differentiate its output?			
What costs would the customer incur if he/she switched to a competitor?			
Are there substitutes to what the SME currently sells?			
What is the ratio of SMEs to the number of customers?			
Are customers price sensitive? Why?			
Is the SME's product or service a "big ticket" or a "grocery" item to the customer?			
How unique is the SME's product or service? Is it distinguishable from others'?			
How customer-friendly is the SME's product or service compared to others'?			
How profitable are the customers?			

6.5.2 Analysing the Threats of New Entrants to the SME's Industry

The attractiveness of an industry and its profitability is influenced by the ease in which competitors enter the industry, or the ease of introduction of a new brand of product which will compete with the SME's products. It is important that the SME attempts to forecast potential new entrants to the industry. Most importantly, the SME should appreciate that every new entry has the potential to take away one or two customers. Where there are barriers to entry due to high start-up capital, access to technology, patents, or state legislation or government policy, the SME would benefit from such industry. Conversely, if it is a free ride for all, the SME will struggle to survive, let alone prosper, unless it manages to develop solutions to the challenges. In fact, the SME sector in Africa has an extremely porous border: entry and exit are very easy, even by foreigners. The story of Chinese chicken farmers competing with local Zambian housewives is a case in point. However, within the context of spirituality and poverty reduction, collaboration with new entrants can offer a better option for meeting the purpose of the business rather than competing. It is worth pointing out that if it is a new industry, new entrants will generate more business that translates into positive synergy. SMEs should always be on the lookout for positive synergy. SMEs in Africa do not enjoy projection of any kind apart from the cartel; they manage to organize themselves. The absence of established regulatory institutions on the continent ensures that the African SME sector is one of the most competitive in the world. Survival is not an easy objective to achieve for any SME start-up in Africa. This is further exacerbated by blind and ill-conceived fierce competition amongst SME operators instead of collaboration. Within the context of spirituality and poverty reduction, collaboration as a strategy is a worthwhile option to consider by all SME operators. For example, the formation of cooperatives amongst those operating in the agricultural sector can play a significant role in poverty reduction.

6.5.3 Analysing the Bargaining Power of the SMEs' Suppliers

Most SMEs in developing countries play the role of *middlemen* in the value chain. Apart from those operating in the service industry, few actually produce what they sell. This means that they rely heavily on suppliers for their inputs. As customers to those suppliers, SMEs need to assess their bargaining strength relative to the suppliers. More specifically,

SMEs need to examine their degree of dependency on the suppliers. SMEs must determine the influence of their suppliers to set the terms of the relationship. For example, they need to know whether their suppliers have the power to influence the volume or price of the commodity or the nature of the service they can provide. There are a few pointers that SMEs can initially use to determine their own relative influence over the suppliers. The first pointer is the number of suppliers available. In situations where there are few suppliers, the SME will have less influence. The second pointer is whether it is easy to switch to another supplier without cost. The third pointer is the uniqueness of the supply (i.e. the product) or the uniqueness of the supplier. For example, a supplier who supplies a unique product of high quality (e.g. a secret formula) can have a significant influence. Similarly, a supplier who has cultivated a certain image or acquired it through accreditation or certification can have some influence in setting the terms of the business relationship. In all cases, the SME needs information. Within an African context, such information is not readily available. Perhaps this lack of data will open up a business opportunity for some unemployed graduate in Economics or Business Management. At any rate, hard or soft data needs to inform a decision about the implications of the status of the SME vis-a-vis the supplier. One of the significant implications of the relative power of the suppliers in an industry is that such power tends to limit the profitability of the industry. Therefore, information on the power of the suppliers can help in making decisions on whether to launch a start-up in such an industry and in some cases whether to quit the industry.

6.5.4 Analysing the Threat of a Substitute to an SME's Products and Services

SME operators can easily make the mistake of thinking that their competitors are those who sell the same product or service. The reality is that, sometimes the most serious competitors are those who do not stock the types of product that SMEs sell or produce. There are those which sell or produce alternatives to the SMEs' products or services. These are called substitutes. In other words, they are products that replace the need for the SMEs' products or services altogether. An industry that has many threats or an imminent threat of a substitute would be less profitable and the SMEs should develop appropriate strategies. SMEs that are involved in transportation or in retailing farm-based agricultural products are more likely to be victims of substitutes. This is because there are many alternatives to a means of transportation and food products in Africa.

Some of these alternatives might be free in certain localities. Therefore, those operators thinking of starting up in such industries need to prepare for such threats and potential low profitability. There are three key criteria for assessing the threat of a substitute. The first criterion is the price performance of the alternative product. This means, would the customer get the same quality of product or service at the same or a lower price at the SME? This also assumes that the customer is privy to information about price and capable of making an informed decision. Given the kinds of customers that most SMEs serve in Africa, slight changes in price can convince a customer to switch to an alternative product or service. The second criterion is switching the cost to the customer who might decide to buy an alternative product or service elsewhere. Again, many of the products and services provided by the SMEs in Africa have limited switching costs, because SMEs have limited room to tie customers legally or otherwise. The third criterion is customer loyalty. Loyal customers are crucial to profitability in any industry because loyalty reduces the expense of marketing efforts. However, keeping them loyal is a challenge when there are substitutes around. It is important for SMEs to understand the level of "promiscuity" of customers in the industry. Within the African context where most industries are less established compared to other parts of the world, customer loyalty is low. This is coupled by the fact that the customer base is young and impressionable. Table 6-7 presents a template for analysing the threats of substitutes to SMEs' products and services.

Table 6-7. Template for Analysing the Threats to the SMEs' Products and Services

	Risk Potential		
	Very Likely	Likely	Unlikely
The likelihood that alternative products or services will be better priced at the same or higher quality than the SMEs'			
The likelihood that the SMEs' customers will incur no cost if they switch to alternative products or services			
The likelihood that the SMEs' customers will try alternative products or services			
The likelihood that the SMEs' customers will switch to alternative products or services			

6.5.5 Analysing Rivalry amongst SMEs

The profitability of the SME's industry will be influenced by the rivalry amongst the existing SMEs. It is natural that every SME will try to acquire more customers and generate more revenue. In other words, SMEs will try to acquire market share even if they do not say so or perhaps do not understand the concept. Also, some SMEs within the industry will try to grow their business. Given that the number of customers is finite, growing business means getting customers from somewhere within the existing industry; hence the growing rivalry amongst the existing players in the industry. How would an SME notice that a fellow SME is trying to pinch its customer? This can be noticed through price competition, an increase in advertising or publicity, and differentiation through customer service to make the SME more attractive. In African culture where personal and social relationships are important, customer service can be a very good weapon for achieving market share. Would-be entrepreneurs and start-ups will be required to understand the degree of rivalry amongst SMEs in the industry. This will help them to make the right decisions and preparations to "move in". Donors and state interventionists who wish to help the youth and unemployed would need to appreciate that some industries are more difficult than others for starting a business, especially for the young and inexperienced. Therefore, knowledge of that should help in the allocation of resources for poverty reduction. There are many pointers that will indicate the degree of rivalry amongst SMEs. Naturally, the greater the rivalry the less profitable the industry would be (Porter, 1980). The first pointer is the rate of growth in the industry. An industry in its infancy will have room for most SMEs; therefore the level of rivalry will be relatively low. Conversely, an old or declining industry will have limited room for existing players, hence there will be high rivalry amongst the players. Another pointer to rivalry is the degree of fixed costs associated with running the business. Where the fixed cost is very high, competitors are trapped and cannot get out, even though the industry is not profitable. They will hang on in there and compete. Where SMEs cannot easily differentiate their product or service then rivalry is likely to be fierce. This is typical of SMEs on the African continent especially those involved in retailing and providing a standard service. Closely related to the issue of differentiation is the question of brand. Here we refer to brand loosely to relate to the industry and sub-industry. If the industry is a strong brand and the customers have a strong brand preference, then the rivalry will be low. Unfortunately, only a few industries in Africa in which SMEs are operating, have strong brands. The specialised business support service is one of them. Also, the brand preferences of African customers in certain products cannot be determined partly because their purchasing power is low, and some industries are not fully established. According to Porter (1980) if an industry is made of players who compete only in that industry, then they are likely to have a great commitment to the industry and will remain in the industry regardless of the challenge. This would mean a high risk of industry rivalry since few are willing to quit the industry. Related to this is the issue of the exit barrier. Where it is difficult to exit the industry due to legal or cost factors, competitive rivalry is going to be high. Another factor that can lead to rivalry amongst SMEs is information complexity (Porter, 1980). The rivalry amongst SMEs is likely to be high if the products of the industry are easily understood.

6.6 Identifying what Determines the Success of the Industry

Knowing what makes a business successful is part of the strategic planning process. SMEs should not decide on the "path" to follow without taking into account the "traditions" that guide the choice. One of the key issues that should be highlighted in entrepreneurship training is that in every category of business there are issues or variables which the SME operator can control. Some of these issues and variables are so important that failure to control them can lead to peril. In other words, the efficiency and effectiveness of control will determine the success of the business. The factors are what experts called *Key Success Factors* (KSFs). SMEs would need to focus on KSFs and exploit them to the maximum in order to succeed in their mission of poverty reduction. Unfortunately, due to some cultural and religious factors, many SME operators in Africa tend to rely on supernatural power only as the key success factor, ignoring the other side which requires an individual effort to demonstrate the seriousness to the supernatural power. This effort means studying the KSFs and developing an appropriate strategy before calling on the help of the supernatural power.

What are the KSFs? There are generic KSFs which have varying degrees of importance depending on the circumstances in which the SME finds itself, the industry in which it is operating, and even the country and region it is operating in. It is therefore important for the SME operator and prospective entrepreneurs in Africa to be aware of the key determinants of success in the industry they are operating in. It is not enough to rely on the research and literature from developed countries as the basis of identifying KSFs in a particular African country, regardless of the industry. Having said that, the SME can use the generic KSF in Table 6-4 as a starting point for examining and determining the KSFs for its own industry in particular and, for SMEs in the African country in general. The industry analysis discussed in the previous section should help the SME determine the elements of the KSFs.

Table 6-4. Determining the Key Success Factors

Generic elements of KSFs	How Critical is this variable?	Now What?
Capital Outlay		
Cost Management		
Location		
Quality		
Customer Service		
Brand Image		
Human Resource Management		
Dependable Suppliers		
Relationship with Local Authority		
Collaboration		
Innovation		
Access to Credit		
Availability of Power Supply		
Experience in the Industry		
Inventory Control		

6.7 Strategic Options for Poverty Reduction

The goal of strategic analysis discussed earlier is to help the SME determine its strengths and weaknesses, as well as the opportunities for the business. The analysis should also help to identify any threats that can challenge the prosperity and survival of the business. Based on the analysis, the SME can set new strategies that help it deliver its vision and mission pertaining to poverty reduction. Porter (1980) has identified three main options available to any business when it is considering how to deal with the competition. SMEs can consider such options. The options are:

Cost Leadership. This is where the SME can try to compete on the basis of cost only. In other words, it will try to produce and deliver goods or services to the customer at a lower cost than its competitor. Although it might decide to charge its customers a lower price than its competitors, this is not necessary. The key strategy is operating at a lower cost than its competitors, not to undercut competitors in terms of price; although cost leadership invariably leads to competitive pricing. Within the African context where purchasing power is very low, cost leadership should be an attractive option for the SME. Adopting this strategy should allow the SME to charge a competitive price, and above all, help the community, which cannot afford to pay a premium price. In other words, cost leadership strategy is in line with poverty reduction. More specifically, an SME that manages its costs effectively is doing a service to the community almost directly. Also, by managing its costs effectively, it can afford to hire more of the unemployed and pay decent wages. Conversely, if the SME cannot manage its costs, it might have to charge higher prices, reduce the workforce and pay lower wages in order to survive.

Differentiation Strategy: This strategy is on the opposite side of a cost leadership strategy. This strategy focuses on providing a product or service that is unique, which allows the SME to charge higher prices. This is also called innovation strategy. An SME can be innovative not in the products they sell; since most African SMEs are retailers; but in other aspects of marketing such as packaging, delivery, customer service, after-sales service, etc. Within the context of poverty reduction, this strategy can also help the community by targeting only the well-off for such a strategy, i.e. those who can afford to pay for the premium product or service. Charging a premium price can help the SME remain in business and continue to employ people who otherwise would have been unemployed. However, it is imperative that the SME markets its strategy to its customers by indicating that they are not only getting premium products and services, but they are also serving the community through supporting the business.

Focus Strategy: This strategy is about targeting a segment of the market. An SME can specialise in a smaller niche market or customers, because either it cannot afford to serve the whole market, because the target market is more lucrative and offers a better opportunity, or has less threats to the business. At any rate, this strategy can have its own risk because it means making a judgement on which segment of the customers to ignore and which to focus on. In a business environment where information and data required to make an informed decision are hard to come by, focus strategy can be a trial-and-error strategy. In fact, that is why focus strategy is not popular amongst SMEs in Africa, especially those in the informal sector (Kigundu,.....). Many, if not most SMEs in sub-Saharan Africa, operate across multiple segments and multiple sectors. Such an approach can also be ineffective because it leads to the loss of specialization, expertise and missed opportunities.

Having developed the option, the next step is to draw up a plan of action and to implement the strategy. This will be the subject of the next chapter.

6.8 Competition versus Collaboration

It is perhaps appropriate to conclude this chapter by tempering enthusiasm for competitive strategy with the virtues of collaboration. Although this chapter focused on the need for the SME to develop strategies in order to compete, *naked competition* will not achieve the objective of poverty reduction. This is particularly the case in an African context where there are no effective institutions to check the excesses of competition. In fact, naked competition is at odds with the system thinking and spirituality advocated in this book. *Naked competition* should be "clothed" with the virtues of spirituality and system thinking. Indeed, the recognition of the ills of unchecked competition is a responsibility for the establishment of watchdogs called competition boards or a competition commission in most developed countries. Conversely, the prevalence of unchecked and unguided competition is responsible for an unproductive SME sector in Africa. In other words, the lack of collaboration and a "*go it alone*" mentality in setting up and running SMEs in Africa leads to a limited return on the time and money invested in the business. A go it alone approach lacks the economy of scale that can generate an adequate return from the business. As a result, the best way to describe many or even most of the businesses in the SME sectors, particularly those in the informal sector, is as businesses that subsidise the economy and the customer. For example, in the agricultural and retail sectors, many SME operators are operating on meagre capital that can hardly be described as start-up capital at all.

6.8.1 Developing a Collaborative Advantage

In line with the system thinking and spirituality advocated in the book, we hereby advocate the need for a collaborative strategy rather than a competitive strategy. In fact, within the African context, we argue that a collaborative strategy should take precedence over a competitive strategy. A competitor analysis and a SWOT analysis can be the starting points for the collaborative strategy. This is because such analyses will enable the identification of potential collaborators based on the analysis of the strengths, potential opportunities and threats that they can pose to the business.

6.9 Conclusion

Reading through this chapter might give the impression that SMEs are required to undertake an extensive and elaborate analysis of the business environment, in fact even large businesses seldom go through such an elaborate process. The aim of this chapter is to help SME operators understand some of the issues that they must take into account to make their businesses successful. Most importantly, policy makers and SME advisers and trainers are supposed to be familiar with the key areas that need to be analysed formally or informally using "soft data".

CHAPTER SEVEN

BUSINESS PLANNING AND MANAGEMENT TOOLS

7.1 Introduction

The previous chapter presented a discussion on the essence of SMEs within the context of poverty reduction in Africa. The chapter particularly highlighted the importance of understanding the mission and purpose of the business within the context of poverty reduction. The chapter also discussed the importance of developing a strategy for the business. However, the chapter did not discuss how the strategy can be implemented and what methods or tools can be used to implement the strategy. Therefore, the purpose of this chapter is to present the techniques and tools for the implementation of a business strategy. The most important and widely-acknowledged method for implementing a business strategy for SMEs is a business plan. The business plan should provide more details on how the strategy is going to work and the resources required to make it work. The business plan can also provide indicative outcomes of the implementation of the strategy. This can help in making critical business decisions before the implementation.

7.2 Business Plan

In this book, business planning is distinguished from strategic planning discussed in the previous chapter. The latter dealt with the essence of the SME as a business, its vision and the broad long-term perspective of how to achieve it. The former, which is the focus of this chapter deals with the operational aspects of the strategy identified in the previous chapter. It provides the day-to-day to-do-list that the business should have to achieve its mission and vision of poverty reduction. Therefore, this chapter should help the entrepreneur develop a business plan for the SME. The business plan for the SME serves as a road map as well as a milestone to be followed in the implementation of the strategy. A business plan, especially one targeted at international, state and local donors should be an elaborate written document. It should describe what the business is about (e.g. transportation, hotel, restaurant, health centre, hair/body grooming), how it can contribute to poverty reduction (e.g. job creation or decent wages), the historical background (when it was set up or when it will start operating), the kinds of customer needs that it satisfies, the current and projected operating results (e.g. jobs created, sales and profit), and the resources used or required to run the business successfully. The business plan is also a document that describes components of the business or the key business processes that deliver the products or services (i.e. the main functional areas). These key business processes might include primary activities such as sourcing of inputs (i.e. inbound logistics), processing the inputs (operation), distribution (outbound logistics), marketing the products and servicing to ensure the functionality of the product as well as customer loyalty. Secondary activities that support the primary activities might also be included in the business plan. These might include human resource activities, the management information system, the infrastructure and and procurement activities (Porter, 1985). Other important elements that should be included in the plan, especially if the plan is needed for seeking funding, are risk assessment, financing, and timelines against goals. In a nutshell, a business plan should be considered as a tool for securing support from outsiders as well as a tool for providing direction to the business and its members.

7.3 The Need for a Business Plan for the SME

The old adage goes *by failing to plan, one is planning to fail*. One cannot overestimate the importance of planning in any of life's endeavours, especially business. There is perhaps nowhere that planning is more needed, and yet is much more difficult to achieve, than in Africa. This is simply because the environment is more unpredictable than in most regions of the world. Also, the institutional structures necessary to support the implementation of any plan are fragile at best. Nonetheless, these are not excuses to avoid planning. In fact, there is no credible alternative as far as African SMEs are concerned. Planning does not have to be formal and elaborate, especially in the case of informal micro-businesses in Africa. However, key questions need to be asked and answered. Once that is done, then the business has some sort of plan. Hodgetts and Kuratko (2010) have offered the key questions that every business plan should ask and answer. They are: where am I going? How will I get there? What opportunities and problems will I run into along the way? How will I deal with them? They also argue that a business plan is a *road map* for the SME and any prospective entrepreneur. It is important to note that plans are not cast in stone. They can and should change because the situation or the environment changes. However, it provides a starting point for the journey. In fact, without a plan it is unlikely that even the closest friend or family member will lend you the funds you need to start a business. The bank, the state and international donors will certainly not listen to any request for financial support without an accompanying business plan. Another point worth noting is that a plan is only as good as its execution. A plan that is not implemented is worse than a blank piece of paper, because the latter can be used to write on.

7.4 The Imperative of a Business Plan for Poverty Reduction

This book is not just about SMEs and entrepreneurship. It is a book with a distinctive goal–poverty reduction through the effective management of African SMEs so they can create jobs and pay decent wages. Therefore, the business plan is imperative for the achievement of such a goal. Although we advocated the virtues of spirituality and system thinking in the previous chapters, those virtues cannot materialize without hard-nosed old-fashioned planning. This is because ideas need to be acted upon otherwise they are just ideas. We have to emphasize this point because so often in an African context, due to embedded spirituality, people sit back and expect *miracles from above*. The concept of spirituality advocated in this book is not a substitute for hard work. Hard work starts with planning, otherwise it will be a waste of time and resources. It is just too risky and stressful to find out what works and what does not work through trial and error. It has also been advocated that key members of the business should participate at the appropriate level in the business planning process. This is because the entrepreneur does not have a monopoly on ideas. Unfortunately, African culture, which tends to be hierarchical and low-trust oriented, does not encourage active participation. However, we believe true entrepreneurs do break through this barrier. Apart from the members of the business, external advice is also necessary. Advice could come from fellow business people as well as consultants. As for those in the same industry, unless the concept of system thinking and spirituality is embraced, the sharing of ideas is not likely to happen; yet collaboration amongst SMEs in Africa is needed more than ever.

There are more reasons why a business plan is a necessity, especially when starting a business or seeking funds for an on-going concern. First of all, the business strategy becomes clearer when a business plan is developed. Most often the weaknesses of strategies do not surface until a plan is developed. For example, when answers to WHO, WHEN and HOW are sought in a business plan, the limitations of the business strategy and even the organizational objectives become obvious. So, drawing up a business plan allows the entrepreneur to critically analyse organizational strategy, objectives and the means of achieving them.

Drawing up a business plan also allows the entrepreneur to undertake a more thorough analysis of the business environment and make an objective judgement regarding the potential of the business to achieve the goal of poverty reduction. We want to emphasize here that the business is not just about making money for the entrepreneur; it is about making money through serving the community. Therefore, any assessment of the viability of the business should be done within this context. A business that will make money for the entrepreneur but not serve the community is unlikely to be sustainable and to contribute to poverty reduction, and therefore is not within the scope or remit of this book. SMEs that expect, or would request some support from the state, NGOs or international donors, will need to develop a plan to demonstrate their commitment, their capacity and ability to operate the enterprise and most importantly, their capacity to contribute to poverty reduction. Similarly, for those SMEs who have benefited from external support in the past, a business plan might be required for the evaluation of the business as a project or intervention for poverty reduction. As we shall see later in this chapter, a business plan should set measurable objectives and targets (e.g. jobs to be created). Such objectives and targets can be used for tracking the progress or otherwise of the business and the performance of people within it. So, a business plan is a tool for measuring performance. A business plan is also a communication tool and guide for the business (Hodgetts and Kuratko, 2010).

7.5 Writing the Business Plan

The business plan should be an important document that captures what the business is about and what the business is doing or will be doing to achieve its goals. Therefore, the document should provide a clear structure of the key aspects of the business so that both internal and external stakeholders will understand how the business is being run or how it is going to be run. The document should at least have the following sections: an Executive Summary; a Description of What Business the SME is involved in; the Key functional/Business process areas; a Risk Assessment; the location; and the Timeframe for major activities/goals.

7.5.1 Executive Summary

The business plan should have an executive summary as the first main element of the content of the document. It is a significant element that provides the substance of the document but most importantly, the essence of what the business is about. From the point of view of "SMEs for poverty reduction", the executive summary should give an idea about the potential of the business to contribute to poverty reduction from the outset. If the business plan is aimed at seeking funding from donors or state agencies, the executive summary must make an interesting read and capture the interest of the potential donor or state agency. Colourful language that might distract from the message should be avoided. Focus more on the substantive issues such as the key elements of the plan. In particular focus on What, How, Why, and Where. Please note, the executive summary is written after the plan has been written.

7.5.2 Business Description

Having presented the executive summary, the next important segment is the description of the business. This segment should provide more details of the business such as its name or proposed name; when it was established or when it will be established; the types of products or services it will be trading in and where. An important aspect of the description of the business should include some description of the industry and where the business is or will be located. This will provide an indication of its profitability as well as its potential for job creation. The distinctive nature of the business should be clearly described to help the donors or funders get a sense of why they should support the enterprise. Sometimes, the selling point of the business could be the entrepreneur himself/herself. However, he/she has to convince himself/herself whether he/she is the selling point. What is it about his/her story or his/her track record that can make the business proposal a success?

7.5.3 Business Processes (Activities)

This section should provide full details of the "value creation" activities. It can use Porter's Value Chain framework to describe the key business processes for delivering the product or service to the customer. It might not necessarily include all the key processes, such as the processing of the inputs, unless it will be a means of convincing the funders or donors regarding the uniqueness of the production activities. Sometimes, donors and funders need to be convinced that the entrepreneur has the capacity and know-how to produce the products at the expected quantity and quality. Therefore, the description of the business process should include the *production/processing* aspects of the business.

Another key aspect of the business plan will include information about the *Market*. There should be a clear description of the structure of the target market. This should include its size, growth, key competitors in the market, and the existing competing products or services in the market. There should be a clear description of how the competition will be handled. There should be clear marketing plans that demonstrate the pricing, the packaging of the product or service, its distribution and the advertising or publicity approach.

The next important segment of the business plan is the *Management Dimension*. Funders and donors want to know who will be running the business operation and who is or who will be making the strategic decisions. The legal structure of the business should be provided. Is it a registered business? Is it a partnership or sole-ownership? Etc. This information is also useful for the regulatory and supporting agencies that support SME development. The number of employees and how they are remunerated should be clearly spelt out. This information is very important, because within the context of poverty reduction, donors and state agencies would like to see an indication of job creation and the salary/wages that could improve the standard of living of the people in the community. There should also be an indication of the type of employment agreements pertaining to wages, training, apprenticeships, etc. Even if the business is a one-man show, there should be a clear statement of how much the entrepreneur will be taking as his/her salary. There must be a clear distinction between the business and the owner-operator in terms of the funds generated through the business. To achieve this distinction, the owner-operator should allocate himself/herself a salary package beyond which he/she cannot go. The management team should also state any kind of external advisory support for the entrepreneur/business. Within the African context, free advisors are not in short supply. However, many advisors, paid or otherwise, do not have the track record or credibility to offer useful advice. Therefore, the SME must be careful about those offering advice.

The next, and most important information that constitutes the business plan is the *Financial Information*. To many stakeholders, this is perhaps the most important information that the plan provides. This is because financial information provides an indication of whether other aspects of the plan are credible and will work or are working. Having a marketing plan and a good management team will not appeal to donors and funders if the financial information indicates that the business is not making money or will not make money. From the poverty reduction perspective, state agencies and international donors will question the prospects of poverty reduction through job creation or decent wages if the business is not making money or will not make money.

What kind of information is needed in the business plan? First of all, the business needs to provide information on the assets and liabilities currently held. The next requirements are the financial projections in terms of sales revenue, and costs (cash flow), which should ultimately demonstrate the profitability of the business. Projected material, labour and overhead costs need to be provided (budget). These should be based on realistic estimates. It is also important to describe the required sources of funds and the uses for which the funds are intended. Also, it is important to demonstrate the stages of financing the business enterprise. This will enable funders, donors and perhaps investors to evaluate the viability of the project at the different stages of its development. In a nutshell, the information in this section should produce pro-forma financial statements. Remember that the information provided in the marketing plan has to tally with the financial forecasting information, otherwise the business plan will be ripped to shreds by those analysing the business plan. If the business plan is for internal consumption, rather than for donors, funders or state agencies, it is imperative that the entrepreneur does not deceive himself/herself by painting a rosy picture of a business which does not exist and might never exist.

Another key element of the business plan is the *Risk Analysis*. In the past a risk assessment has not been part of a business plan. However, more recently, especially due to the turbulent economic environment of the last two decades, risk analysis and risk management have become critical parts of business management. This is not to suggest that the issue of risk has not been important to entrepreneurs and investors. If anything, when people assess a business plan they have always been assessing the degree of risk involved although such is not always made explicit. SMEs and entrepreneurs should not shy away from pointing out the potential risks involved. By pointing out the potential risks, it will demonstrate to funders, donors and supporting agencies that they have the capacity to notice challenges and deal with them appropriately. Failure to point to the potential risks will highlight that they (i.e. the entrepreneurs) are a very risky proposition to invest in. Some of the areas of risk that need to be highlighted will relate to the competition, the supply of input materials and energy, reliance on few technically skilful people, industry-wide trends, the influence of family members, corruption, state intervention, civil and communal unrest, missed sales projections, escalating costs, etc. In all these areas, the entrepreneurs must demonstrate how the risks will be tackled if they occur. The whole idea of risk analysis is to uncover potential problems before they occur and plan how to deal with them. Although the African business environment can be one of the riskiest in the world due to the lack of stable institutions, many business operators do not analyse risk or its level before and during running a business. For example, many do not know the original source of their input until they run out of supplies. Many are not aware of any government policy that might enable or constrain their business.

There are also equally important elements that need to be included in the business plan that might fall outside the key business process or value chain. The first is the *Location*. The business plan should clearly demonstrate where the business will be located and why the business is located there. Through analysis of the location's advantages and disadvantages, the business/entrepreneur will identify some risks and how to deal with them. Some of the advantages of location might be to do with the proximity to customers, the source of energy and other inputs, the proximity to transportation and security, etc. These advantages need to be highlighted in the business plan to convince donors and suppliers. The costs associated with the location must also be highlighted. For the purpose of poverty reduction, the proximity to unemployed centres can be a selling point to donors and funders. As we explained in the previous chapter, a business is not set up just to make money. In fact, the purpose of any business is not to make money but to service customers and other stakeholders. If it serves its customers well, then it will make money.

The second element that might not be a key business process for a typical African SME is *Research and Development*. Here, we are not necessarily talking about developing new products since most SMEs are retailers. It is imperative that the business plan demonstrates that the entrepreneur has innovative capacity or potential, especially in the area of accessing new markets and suppliers, developing new processes, new customer service systems, etc. SMEs in the service industry, such as tailoring, hair grooming and restaurants, need to demonstrate that they have the capacity to come up with new designs, new recipes, etc.

The third element of the business plan after presenting the key business activities is the *Milestone*. This is a clear timetable of the major phases of the venture. It should specify the objectives and the activities to achieve the objectives as well as the timeframe for the activities.

Table 7-1. Template for the Structure of a Business Plan

Key Sections	Description
Executive Summary	Provides the substance of what the business is about. From the point of view of "SME for poverty reduction", the executive summary should give an idea about the potential of the business to contribute to poverty reduction from the outset. If the business plan is aimed at seeking funding from donors or state agencies, the executive summary must make interesting reading and capture the interest of the potential donor or state agency.
Business Description	Provide details of the business such as its name or proposed name; when it was established or when it will be established; the types of products or services it will be trading in and where; include some description of the industry and where the business is or will be located.
Business Processes	
Management Dimension	Provide the legal structure of the business (e.g. Is it a registered business? Is it a partnership or sole-ownership? etc.). Provide an indication of the number of employees and how they are remunerated. Provide information on the organizational structure (e.g. sections of the business, managerial and employee structure as well as their specialisation).
Financial Information	Provide information on the assets and liabilities; financial projections in terms of sales revenue, costs (cash flow); projected material, labour and overhead costs need to be provided (budget); describe the required sources of funds and the uses for which the funds are intended; demonstrate the stages of financing the business enterprise.
Risk Analysis	Explain the potential risks associated with the business venture and how you intend to mitigate the risks.
Location	Explain where the business will be located and why the business is located there.
Research and Development	Demonstrate that you have the innovative capacity especially in the area of accessing new markets and suppliers, developing new processes, new customer service systems, etc.
Milestone	Timetable of the major phases of the business venture.

7.6 Strategic and Operational Tools for Managing SMEs

There are several strategic management tools that SMEs can use for long-term planning for their business. Some were mentioned earlier (SWOT analysis). The intention of this section is to elaborate on the tools and suggest how SMEs in Africa can use them or how trainers can help to train entrepreneurs.

The ones that we consider very relevant are: a) Balanced scorecard; b) Value chain; and c) Several diagnostic questionnaires (e.g. organizational climate, organizational culture, organizational satisfaction, etc.). These tools can enable researchers not only to determine the type and level of SME capability, but also its impact on stakeholders and the poor. In a nutshell, these tools can enable SME operators to assess the business' ability to meet the objectives. The following sections elaborate on what these tools are and how they can be used.

Balance Scorecard: A balance scorecard is a management tool for research as well as a practice that enables the investigation of how business objectives and strategy can be translated into action. Specifically, it enables the examination of the relationship between internal processes and external outcomes (Kaplan & Norton, 1996). A balance scorecard argues that organizations should be viewed from four perspectives: 1) Learning and growth perspectives; 2) the Business process perspective; 3) the Customer perspective; and 4) the Financial perspective.

Kaplan & Norton (1996) are of the view that metrics should be developed for each perspective, and data should be collected and analysed for each. Several researchers have applied a balance scorecard and found it to be a useful tool (see, Chow; Haddad & Williamson, 1997; Olve; Petri; Roy & Roy, 2004; Olson & Slater, 2002; Berkman, 2002; Schay; Beach; Caldwell & Lapolice, 2002). For an SME, the use of this tool should be modified to capture its constituencies and its mission for poverty reduction. Therefore, we suggest the following modification. We suggest that SMEs should be viewed from four perspectives: 1) the External stakeholders' perspective; 2) the perspective of internal organizational processes; 3) the Learning and growth perspective; and 4) the Target Beneficiary (the poor) perspective. The metrics below demonstrate how the perspectives can be analyzed in relation to the SME's mission and goals. As can be seen, each perspective should address specific simple questions: a) how do activities contribute to customers' satisfaction? b) How do internal activities and processes add value to the target beneficiaries and customers? c) Are SMEs learning, changing and improving in the light of the changes in priorities? d) How well do SMEs serve their target market?

For each of the four perspectives, SMEs should examine whether they have established targets, how they measure them, what the outcomes are, and what initiatives/actions are to be taken to achieve the desired outcomes.

Table 7-2. Balance Scorecard for SMEs

Perspective	Key question	Target	Measure	Outcome	Initiative
Customers	How do SMEs' activities contribute to customers' satisfaction?				
Internal processes	How do internal activities and processes add value to the target beneficiaries and stakeholders?				
Learning & Growth	Are SME's learning, changing and improving in the light of the changes of priorities of the stakeholders and target beneficiaries?				
Target beneficiaries	Do SMEs serve their beneficiaries effectively?				

Value chain analysis (VCA): Although the balanced scorecard can be the main tool to be used in implementing SME strategy, the VCA can be used to complement the analysis of the efficiency of the SME's activities and processes. The VCA is a management tool popularized by Porter (1985) to identify where "value" is added in an organization and links the process with the main functional parts of the organization (Lynch, 2006: 200). Essentially, the VCA splits organizations into primary activities of production and support activities such as human resource management, firm infrastructure, technology and procurement. For SMEs in the service sector rather than the manufacturing organizations, the distinction between primary activities and support activities cannot be easily made. Instead, all activities should be analyzed in terms of their contributions in adding value to the SME, which ultimately add value to the customer. As Lynch (2006) points out, the VCA can be used to identify the cost efficiency of each organizational activity, which then enables the firm to determine the strengths and weaknesses of its operation. The VCA can be used as a means of determining the SME's operational efficiency. Researchers can divide an SME's operations into specific activities/processes and attempt to determine the cost of each discrete activity in terms of time and money.

Both the balance scorecard and the VCA focus entirely on examining the existing resources in terms of capability. No mention is made regarding whether the resources exist and whether they are adequate in terms of quality and quantity. To address this, a resource audit should be undertaken using internal factors and an evaluation matrix technique (David, 2005). This can be in the form of identifying tangible resources in each operation in terms of quantity and quality within the context of the mission and objectives of the SME. Financial, human and technological resources will fall into these categories.

Diagnostic tools: Several questionnaires are available that can be used to examine the SME's environment in terms of systems, structure, climate and culture. Such questionnaires can also be used to examine the experience of the employees and the manager within the organization and its environment. For example, there are leadership style questionnaires, organizational climate and culture questionnaires. Similarly, there are questionnaires that can investigate employees' and customers' satisfaction. Other questionnaires can examine the stakeholder's degree of satisfaction with SMEs.

7.7 Conclusion

This chapter has presented tools and techniques to enable the SME operator to implement the strategy of the business. We devote this concluding part of the chapter to suggest how trainers can train the SME operators to put into practice the ideas presented in the chapter. First, trainers should emphasize the importance of using modern tools and techniques in managing their business. These techniques might appear foreign but in reality, they are common sense approaches practised widely by successful SMEs around the world, including Africa. They are practised using different names and more often without any name. For example, the idea of satisfying the needs of customers and stakeholders advocated in the balance scorecard is not new to successful businesses in

Africa. Similarly, the idea of learning and growth is also not a novel idea. What is novel in modern tools and techniques is that they are packaged coherently to enable the effective running of a business.

Second, trainers should espouse the benefits of planning. The characteristics of the business environment in Africa do not help the entrepreneur to undertake a long-term plan. This is largely due to the constant change, absence of reliable data and absence of strong institutions. Having said that, to be successful, SMEs must have a long-term vision and action plans that will enable the realization of the vision. The plan should be constantly reviewed to reflect the changes in the environment.

Finally, trainers should guide the trainees in developing their business plans. Similarly, they should be guided on how to use the tools and techniques which have been presented in this chapter. We particularly encourage the trainers to focus on the balance scorecard and the VCA. The former will tie in the business strategy as discussed in the previous chapter with the implementation of the strategy through the business plan. The VCA analysis will be useful for determining the effectiveness and efficiency of the resource conversion process.

CHAPTER EIGHT

CONCLUSION

We set out to write a book that would fill a gaping hole in the existing SME books and related materials. We have been motivated and inspired to write this book as a result of personal experience and concern for the underprivileged people in Africa who have been trying to find the means of livelihood through setting up and running their own businesses. We also sympathize with development agencies that have been attempting to support the poor and the unemployed through the provision of entrepreneurship training and the enacting of policies. Although such policies seem appropriate on paper their potency on poverty reduction has been questionable. Having reviewed the existing textbooks and training materials on SME development in Africa, we identified a few issues that require urgent attention in order to improve the potency of the SME policies on poverty reduction. The first weakness in the existing literature is the conceptualization of the policy on using the SME sector as an engine for economic development and poverty reduction. Valid and feasible as it may sound, this approach is compartmentalized along disciplines with economists leading the argument. The issue of poverty in Africa cannot be confined to a single discipline or policy level. The poor are not concerned about where the solutions come from or how they are provided. Most importantly, poverty cannot be solved through setting up a business alone. Therefore, materials written about the ways SMEs can help eradicate poverty and provide employment should cut across disciplines and across policy levels.

The second related weakness is the limited number of books on ways that SMEs can help in poverty reduction. Most significantly perhaps, the existing books are theoretical and academic in nature. They are not targeted at practitioners or policy makers. We believe that enough academic materials exist about the contribution and potential contribution of SMEs in the economy and the eradication of poverty. Attention should now be paid to how the theories can be put into practice. There should be more focus on translating the knowledge created by research into practical solutions. The audience should be policy makers and practitioners, not fellow academics. Africa is in need of practical solutions generated from academic research. More specifically, research should be translated into practical guidelines for poverty reduction in Africa.

Thirdly, the *silo* approach to dealing with poverty reduction neglects a key component which is critical to the successful outcomes in any intervention. The key component is the poor person him/herself. The macro policy approach has largely failed to acknowledge that some people have successfully pulled themselves out of poverty despite the harsh economic, social and cultural environment. Therefore, there is a need to take into account the personal characteristics of the poor when enacting policies. Policies should go through a hierarchy of levels; institutional, organizational and individual. Materials written on reducing poverty should not ignore the individual characteristics of the poor. The current approach seems to suggest that poverty is created by circumstances external to the person. This book counters that argument. The role of external factors is recognised in this book however, individual characteristics are vital in the implementation of poverty reduction interventions.

The fourth weakness identified in the existing literature is the neglect of the socio-cultural context of the African environment. It is widely acknowledged by development experts across most disciplines that culture and traditions enable or constrain the efficacy of national policy. Yet prescriptions and discourse on how SMEs can help in the fight against poverty in Africa are devoid of cultural consideration. Textbooks and materials on how SMEs can help in poverty reduction do not delve into the issues of why and how culture and traditions can impact on the efficacy of national policies targeted at SMEs. Specifically, textbooks on the role of SMEs in Africa do not explain why communities in the same country are better at producing successful entrepreneurs. These weaknesses outlined above set the foundation for writing the book. The following section summarises the themes covered in the book.

8.1 Main Themes of the Book

8.1.1 The Theme of Poverty

The key theme identified and discussed in this book is the notion of poverty. Experts agreed that poverty is multi-dimensional. Poverty consists of income poverty, education poverty, and health poverty. The main causes of poverty in Africa have been largely attributed to sources of income, poor governance, joblessness, ethnic and civil conflict, environmental degradation, and social construction of gender. Several policies have been enacted at international and national levels to address the issue of poverty in Africa. Our point of departure was to challenge the emphasis placed on the external environment as the main cause of poverty.

We advanced the concept of *spiritual poverty* as the foundation of poverty. We argued that there is a human dimension to the enactment and implementation of poverty reduction policy. We argued that *spiritually endowed* policy makers and implementers will enact and implement policies that are appropriate for poverty reduction in Africa. We advocated the use of system thinking in the enactment of poverty reduction policy and its implementation. We drew the implications of spirituality for training and developing policy makers and entrepreneurs in Africa. Similarly, we advocated that SME operators should be oriented to use system thinking and spirituality in their daily activities. The concept of spirituality was chosen as a cornerstone for policy making and implementation because it is a concept that Africans are familiar with, and it is compatible with African culture and tradition. It is a concept that will be easier to understand and be implemented given that it is a neutral concept, but yet compatible with the major religions in Africa.

8.1.2 The Theme of SMEs

The second theme of the book is that of the role of SMEs in job creation. It is clearly demonstrated that job creation and poverty reduction can only be addressed through the private sector. Most significantly, the only sector that has the capacity to address the issue of unemployment which should lead to the eradication of most dimensions of poverty is the SME sector. However, it is acknowledged that the SME sector, especially in Africa, faces significant challenges that militate against its capacity to be the engine of economic development and poverty reduction in Africa. Hence, several policies have been enacted to support the sector. However, failure to take an innovative approach to policy formulation and implementation ensures that the policies do not adequately mitigate the challenges faced by SME operators. We returned to the central theme of the book which is spirituality and system thinking to guide the development of appropriate and culture-sensitive policies that will enable the sector to deliver on its potential to address unemployment and poverty on the continent.

8.1.3 The Theme of Spirituality and System Thinking

The cornerstone of this book is the concept of spirituality in business. We adopted the concept of spirituality to provide a point of departure from other books, because it has some key advantages. First, it is a neutral concept that can be easily understood by Africans due to their religiosity. Second, it is a powerful concept that pervades the lives of Africans, both the educated and the uneducated. Third, coupled with the concept of system thinking, it provides a motivational foundation for change in behaviour that can reform policy makers, policy implementers, and business operators. The concept provides practical guidelines and a *to-do-list* pertaining to how people should interpret their circumstances and behave in specific ways to achieve the desired outcomes. The concept acts as a powerful tool for training and developing entrepreneurs.

8.1.4 Personal Development Theme

This theme is one of the key features of the book that has distinguished it from any other book on SMEs. This theme assumes that the practical skills in running a business are not enough to deliver success. The theme addresses the common weaknesses in entrepreneurship training programmes which ignore the characteristics of the trainee in favour of providing the skills in running a business. The theme underscores the importance of personal values and beliefs as a foundation for developing and realising personal goals within the context of poverty eradication. It emphasises the need to set personal goals that are in harmony with societal wellbeing. In line with the notion of spirituality and system thinking, the theme debunks the idea that the hard-nosed pursuit of individualistic economic goals will necessarily lead to a sustainable achievement of poverty reduction in Africa. The theme provided practical guidelines on how to set and achieve personal goals that are in harmony with society, which will ultimately lead to sustainable business success. The latter will depend on the former.

8.1.5 The Theme of Planning and Managing SMEs

The final key theme of the book focused on how to develop a strategic plan for the business. It underscores the need for SMEs to act professionally by using modern tools and techniques for running a business. The theme provided practical tools and techniques that can help trainers and trainees during entrepreneurship training. The theme underscores the importance of the African business environment and the need to take that into account when planning and operating a business. In a nutshell, this theme argues that running an SME in Africa does not have to be different from running it elsewhere, provided that the entrepreneur sets personal and business goals that are in harmony with the society and pursues the goals within the context of the African business environment.

8.2 The Way Forward

What is the way forward regarding using the SME sector as a vehicle for poverty reduction in Africa? The potential of the sector to perform this objective is unquestionable. However, we believe experts who are writing on the topic of SMEs should address the issue of audience. For far too long, Africa has been waiting for guidelines on how the knowledge generated by the researchers on poverty, SMEs and public policy, can be translated into practical solutions for individuals trapped in poverty and hopelessness. There is undoubtedly the need for experts to start focusing their attention on writing materials that can directly help the poor person on the street to benefit from the knowledge generated from research. The interface between research, policy, implementation and the individual needs to be identified and bridged. The notion of interdependence and spirituality has been central to our approach to using SMEs as instruments of poverty reduction. However, because public policy has a significant impact on the efficacy of the sector to address poverty in Africa, the notion of spirituality and interdependence should not be solely confined to entrepreneurship training. Policy makers and implementers should be subjected to specific training programmes that drive home the need to adopt system thinking and spirituality in policy formulation and implementation.

Training programmes should not be confined to technical skills alone. Policy makers and implementers of policy should be subjected to personal development regimes akin to the one offered to would-be entrepreneurs. There should be a total reform of the training and development programs to embrace a personal development model which should lead to appropriate policy formulation and implantation pertaining to the SME sector. Still on the topic of training, given the African tradition and culture, training of entrepreneurs as an intervention for poverty reduction should not be confined to the entrepreneurs alone. Given that the family is central to African life, and family can impact on the successful operation of the business, training programmes should include the family and the community. There should be a sensitization program for the family and the community to appreciate, at the very least, that their influence on the entrepreneur can make or break the business. They should be reoriented to understand that the success of the entrepreneur is their own success; so is the failure of the entrepreneur.

We conclude this book by calling on international development institutions, states, and local governments to initiate a project dedicated to the development of success stories of entrepreneurs in Africa. The case studies should be structured at regional, national, and community levels. Based on the case studies, training programmes should be developed to highlight the ingredients of success. Similarly, there should be a project that celebrates the "success" of entrepreneurs. In line with the notion of spirituality and interdependence, success should not be measured by personal achievement alone. Finally, there should be similar projects for policy makers and implementers that mirror the model in the SME sector.

REFERENCES

Abor J., and Quartey, P., (2010). Issues in SME Development in Ghana and South Africa. *International Research Journal of Finance and Economics*, Issue 39, pp. 218-228

Acs, Z.J. and Audretsch, D.B. (1993). Small Firms and Entrepreneurships: an East-West Perspective. Cambridge University Press, Cambridge, New York, USA

Ahmad, K. (2003).The challenge of global capitalism: An Islamic perspective. In Dunning, J. H. (ed.) *Making globalization good: The moral challenges of global capitalism*. London: Oxford University Press, p.181-209.

Aragón-Sánchez, A. and Sánchez-Marin, G. (2005). Strategic Orientation, Management Characteristics, and Performance: A Study of Spanish SMEs. Journal of Small Business Management, Vol. 43, No. 3, p. 287-308

Africa Commission Report (2005). *Our Common Interest.* London: Office of the Prime Minister, March 2005

Amin, A. (2004). The Distributional Role of Small Business in Development. International Journal of Social Economics, Vol. 31, No. 4, p. 970-383

Apter, M.J (1985). Religious state of mind: A reversal theory interpretation. In L.B. Brown (ed.). *Advances in Psychology of Religion.* 62-75. Oxford: Pergamon Press

Aryeetey, E. and Ahene, A.A. (2005). Changing Regulatory Environment For Small-Medium Size Enterprises And Their Performance In Ghana, Centre on Regulation and Competition Working Paper Series, Paper No. 103. Available at: www.competition-regulation.org.uk/publicat ions/working_papers/wp103.pdf.

Ashar, H & Lane-Maher, M. (2004). Success and Spirituality in the New Business Paradigm. *Journal of Management Inquiry*, September 2004 vol. 13 no. 3 249-260

Aterido, Reyes, Mary Hallward-Driemeier & Carmen Pages (2009), Big Constraints to Small Firms' Growth? Business Environment and Employment Growth across Firms, *World Bank Policy Research Working Paper* 5032 (Washington DC: World Bank)

Audretsch, D.B. and Klepper, S. (2000). Innovation, Evolution of Industry and Economic Growth. Elgar Reference Collection. International Library of Critical Writings in Economics. Cheltenham, U.K. and Northampton, Mass.

Australian Agency for International Development (AusAID) (2001), Reducing poverty — the central integrating factor of Australia's Aid Program

Ayyagari.M, Beck. T. and Demirirguc-Kunt., A. (2005), Small and Medium Enterprises across the Globe. Available at: http://siteresources.worldbank.org/DEC/Resources/84797-1114437274304/SME_globe.pdf.

Banathy, B.H. (1991). Cognitive mapping of educational systems for future generations. *WorldFutures,* 31:5-17.

Banathy, B.H. (1996). *Designing social systems in a changing world.* New York: Plenum Press

Bateson, G. (1979). *Mind and nature: A necessary unity.* New York: Ballentine

Baumeister, R.F. and Exline, J.J. (1999). Virtue, Personality, and Social Relations: Self-Control as the Moral Muscle. *Journal of Personality* , Volume 67, Issue 6, pages 1165–1194,

Beaver, G. and Carr, P., (2002), "The Enterprise Culture: Understanding a Misunderstood Concept". Journal of Strategic Change, Vol.11, No.2, p105-113.

Beck, Thorsten, and Asli Demirguc-Kunt, A. (2004). "SMEs, Growth, and Poverty." *Public Policy for the Private Sector, Note 268.* World Bank, Washington, DC.

Beck, T, Demirguc-Kunt, A, and Levine, R. (2005). "SMEs, Growth, and Poverty: A Working Paper," 11224

Berkman, 1. (2002). Social Determinants of Health: Meeting at the Cross-soads. *Health Affairs.* March 2002 vol. 21 no. 2291-293

Berry, S. (1993), No Condition is Permanent: The Social Dynamics of Agrarian Change in sub-Saharan African.The University of Wisconsin Press, Wisconsin, USA

Berry T, T., Sweeting, B., Goto, J. and Taylor, M.(2002), Financial Management Practice Amongst SMEs. Manchester Metropolitan University Business School, Manchester, Working Paper, 02/16

Beyene, A. 2002. Enhancing the competitiveness and productivity of Small and Medium Scale Enterprises (SMMEs) in Africa: an analysis of differential roles of national governments through improved support services. *Africa Development*, 27(3): 130-156.

Bhagwati, J and Srinivasn, T.S.(2002), Trade and Poverty in the Poor Countries. *American Economic Review*. Vol.92, No.2, p.180-183

Biggs, T. (2003). Is Small Beautiful and Worthy of Subsidy? Available at: http://rru.worldbank.org/Documents/PapersLinks/TylersPaperonSMEs. pdf

Birch, D. L. (1979), The job Creation Process, Final Report to Economic Development Administration. Cambridge, MA

Bird, K. (2004), A framework to analyse linkages between trade policy, poverty   reduction   and   sustainable   development.   Overseas Development Institute. Available at http://www.odi.org/sites/odi.org.uk/files/odi-assets/publications-opinion-files/2334.pdf

Blackwood, D.L. and Lynch, R.G. (1994). The measurement of inequality and poverty: A policy maker's guide to the literature. *World Development,* 1994, vol. 22, issue 4, pages 567-578

Booth, D. (2001), PRSP Processes in 8 African Countries: Initial Impacts and Potential for Institutionalisation. Overseas Development Institute, London

Botswana Ministry of Commerce and Industry. (1999), Policy on Small Medium and Micro Enterprises in Botswana. Government Paper No.1. Government Printer, Gaboreone

Boulding, K.E. (1956). General systems theory -- the skeleton of science. Management Science, 2:197-208

Brinkerhoff, D.W. (1999). State-Civil Society Networks For Policy Implementation in Developing Countries. *Review of Policy Research* Volume 16, Issue 1, pages 123–147, March 1999. Abt Associates Inc. Bethesda, Maryland

Brown, C., Medoff, J. and Hamilton, J. (1990). Employers: Large and Small. Cambridge, Harvard University Press. Clarendon Press, Oxford

Burnell, P. (1997). Foreign Aid in A Changing World. Open University Press, Buckingham, Philadelphia

Butts, D. (1999). Spirituality at Work: an Overview. *Journal of Organizational Change Management*, 12(4): 328-331.

Calcopietro, C.M. (1999), Tanzania Small and Medium Scale Enterprise Policy Proposals, Dar es Salaam, Tanzania USA.UNIDO

Calderon, M.C., Chong, A.and Gradstein, M. (2006), Foreign Aid, Income Inequality, and Poverty. Inter-American Development Bank Banco Interamericano de Desarrollo (BID) Research Department Departamento de Investigación *Working Paper 547*. University of Pennsylvania

Callan, T. and Nolan, B. (1991). Concepts of poverty and the poverty line. *Journal of Economic Surveys* 5 (3), 243-261

Carlsson, B (1996). Small Business, flexible technology and industrial dynamics, in Z. Acs, B. Carlsson, and R. Thurik. (eds.). *Small Business in Modern Economy.* Oxford: Blackwell, 63-125

Cavanagh, G.F. (1999). Spirituality for managers: context and critique. *Journal of Organizational Change Management,* Vol. 12 Iss: 3, pp.186 - 199

Caves, R.E. (1998). Industrial Organization and New Findings on the Turnover and Mobility of Firms. Journal of Economic Literature, Vol. 36, No. 4, p.1947-1982

Checkland, P. (1981). *Systems thinking, systems practice.* New York: Wiley

Chow, C. W., K. M. Haddad, and J. E. Williamson. 1997. Applying the balanced scorecard to small companies. *Management Accounting* (August): 21-27.

Chuta, E. and Liedholm, C. (1985) Employment and Growth in Small-Scale Industry: Empirical Evidence and Policy Assessment from Sierra Leone. Macmillan Press LTD, London

Collier, P.and Dollar D. (2001), Can the World Cut Poverty in Half? How Policy Reform and Effective Aid Can Meet Internationla Development Goals. World Development Vol.29, No.11, p.1787-1802

Collier, P. (2009), "Post-Conflict Recovery: How Should Strategies be Distinctive?" *Journal of African Economies* (18), AERC Supplement: i99-i131.

Cooper, C. and Otley, D. (1998), The 1996 Research Assessment Exercise for Business and Management. British journal of Management, Vol.9, No.2, p. 73-89

Cypher, J.M. and Dietz, J.L. (2004). The Process of Economic Development. Routledge; 3Rev Ed edition

Dalberg (2011). Report on Support to SMEs in Developing Countries through Financial Intermediaries. Geneva.

Dana L.P (2007). *Handbook of ethnic minority entrepreneurship: A co evolutionary view of resource management.* London: Edward Elgar

Daniels, L (1994). Changes in the small-scale enterprise sector from 1991 to 1993: Results of a second nationwide survey in Zimbabwe. *GEMINI Technical Report No. 71* PACT Publications, New York (1994)

Davidson, J.C and Caddell, D.P. (1994) Religion and the meaning of work, *Journal for the Scientific Study of Religion,* 33 (2), 135 - 147.

Davidson P and Delmar, F. (2003), Hunting for New Employment: The Role of High Growth Firms.In: Reader, A., Kirby, D.A and Watson, A (eds), Small Firms and Economic Development in Developed and Transition Economies, Ashgate Publising Limited, Germany.p.7-19

Department for International Development (DFID) (2000), Eliminating World Poverty: Making Globalization Work for the Poor, London. White Paper on International Development. Available at: http://www.dfid.gov.uk/pubs/files/whitepaper2000.pdf.

Dyer, W. (2001). 10 Secrets for Success and Inner Peace. Hay House, London

—. (2007). Change *your thoughts, change your life*. Hay House. New York

Easterly, W. (2005). What did structural adjustment adjust? The association of policies and growth with repeated IMF and World Bank adjustment loans. Journal of Development Economics, Vol.2, no.30, p.1-22

The Economic Commission for Africa. (2001), Enhancing the competitiveness of Small and Medium Enterprises in Africa: A Strategic Framework for Institutional Support. Available at: http://www.uneca.org/dpmd/SME%20Strategic%20Framework.pdf

Edgcomb, E and Thetford T (2004). *The informal economy: Making It In Rural America*. The Aspen Institute, United States of America

Eggenberger-Argote, N. (2005), Private Sector Development in the Context of Poverty Reduction Strategy. Discussion Paper Number 1

Ellis, K. (2010) The Private Sector and Development. *ODI, Policy Brief.* May, 2010

Emmons, R.A., Cheung, C. and Tehrani, K. Emmons, (1998). Assessing Spirituality through Personal Goals: Implications for Research on Religion and Subjective Well-Being. *Social Indicators Research*; 45 (1-3), pp. 391-442

Emmons, R. A. (2000). Is spirituality an intelligence? *The International Journal for the Psychology of Religion*, 10, 1–26.

EMPRETEC Ghana Foundation. (2002), Improving the Enabling Environment for Indigenous Private sector Growth and Investment. Ghana Case Study, Department for International Development, Bannock Consulting Ltd

Erastus-Sacharia, A. Hansohm, D and Kadhikwa, G. (1999), Small enterprise support institutions in Namibia NEPRU Research Report NO. 17

Erixon, F. (2005), Aid and development: Will it work this time? International Policy Network, London

Federal Democratic Republic of Ethiopia, Ministry of Trade and Industry. (1997), Micro and Small Enterprises Development Strategy

Feinstein, D., & Krippner, S. (1988). *Personal mythology: The psychology of your evolving self.* Los Angeles, CA: Jeremy P. Tarcher

Fischer, J., (2003). *F&E-Informationssysteme: Hilfsmittel oder Treiber im Innovationsprozess? Arbeitskreis Forschungs- und Entwicklungsmanagement der Schmalenbach-Gesellschaft für* Betriebswirtschaft e.V., Köln-Paderborn.

Fishman, T. (2006). *China Inc: The relentless rise of the next great superpower.* London Simon & Schuster.

Fjose, S; Grunfeld, L.A & Green, C (2010). SMEs and growth in sub-Saharan Africa: Identifying SMEs roles and obstacles to growth. MENON-publication no. 14/2010

Floyd, D. and McManus, J. (2005). The Role of SMEs in improving the Competitive Position of the European Union. European Business Review, Vol.17, No. 2, p. 144-150

Frankel, Jeffrey A., and David H. Romer. 1999. "Does Trade Cause Growth?" *American Economic Review*, 89(3): 379-399

Gardner, H. (1993). *Frames of mind: The theory of multiple intelligences.* New York: Basic Books.

—. (1995, November). Reflections on multiple intelligences: Myths and messages. *Phi Delta Kappan*, 204–207.

—. (1997). *Extraordinary Minds.* New York: Basic Books.

Gauci, A. and Karingi, S. (2007), Trade and Poverty: the little we know of the effect in Africa and possibly why.PEP. IDB Policy Forum on Trade and Poverty. United Nations Economic Commission for Africa

Gebremariam, G.H., Gebremedhin, T.G and Jackson, R.W. (2004). The Role of Small Business in economic Growth and Poverty Alleviation in West Virginia: An Empirical Analysis, Research Paper 2004-10, West Virginia University

Gibb, A.A. (2000) 'Corporate Restructuring and Entrepreneurship: What can large organisations learn from small?', *Enterprise and Innovation Management Studies, 1(1), 19-35.*

Global Poverty Report. (2000), G8 Okinawa Summit

Guillermo P. and Olarreaga, M. (2006), Trade Liberalization, Inequality and Poverty Reduction in Latin America. Paper presented at ABCDE, San Petersburg

Haftendorn, K. (2003), Youth Employment Network-Roadmap for Youth entrepreneurship. International Labour Office. Economic Commission for Europe Coordinating Unit for Operational Activities. Economic and Social. NY. United Nations.

Hagenaars, A and De Vos, K. (1988). The Definition and Measurement of Poverty. *Journal of Human Resources,* Vol. 23, No. 2, p.211-221

Hall, C. (2000), E-Commerce and SMEs in APEC-HRD implications and the role PECC, Paper printed to the 9th annual meeting of PECC-HRD,

Pacific Economic Cooperation Council Human Resources Development Task Force, Taiwan

Hallberg, K. (2000). A Market-Oriented Strategy for Small and Medium-Scale Enterprises. International Finance Corporation, Discussion Paper Number 40, Washington, D.C. World Bank. Available at: http://www.netlibrary.com/Reader/

Hernando de Soto.(1989), Statement made at a symposium on the Informal sector: Issues in Policy Reform and Programme sponsored by the United States Agency for International Development, Abidjan, Ivory Coast

Hodgetts, R.M. and Kuratko, D. (2010). *Entrepreneurship*. Cengage Learning. London

Hoftstede, G. (1991). *Cultures and Organizations: Software of the Mind*. Cambridge, UK: McGraw-Hill.

Hong Kong Trade Development Council, (2012)

House, R.J., Hanges, P.J., Javidan, M., Dorfman, P.W. and Gupta, V. (2004). *Culture leadership and organization: The GLOBE study of 62 societies*. London: Sage

Hulme, D. (2003), Chronic Poverty and development Policy: An Introduction. World Development, Vol.31, No.3, p.399-402

—. (2007). Inclusive globalization: India's role in tackling global poverty, Exim Bank of India Annual Commencement Day lecture 2007, Mumbai, Exim Bank.

Hutanuwatr, P. (1998). *Globalization seen from Buddhist perspective*. In Camilleri, J.A. and Muzaffar C. (eds.) Globalization: The perspectives and experiences of the religious Traditions of Asia pacific, Kuala Lumpur: International Movements for a Just World, p.91-104.

IFAD (2007). Ghana: upper east region land conservation and smallholder rehabilitation Project (LACOSREP), report. Available at: http://www.ifad.org/evaluation/public_html/eksyst/doc/prj/region/pa/g hana/s026ghbe.htm

International Fund for Agricultural Development (IFAD). (2000/2001), *Rural Poverty Report. The Challenge of Ending Rural Poverty*. Oxford University Press, New York

IFAD, (2007). *Private Sector Development and Partnership Strategy*. Rome, Italy

—. (2010). *Rural Poverty Report 2011*, Rome: Rome, Italy.

—. (2011). *Corporate-level evaluation of IFAD's private sector development and partnership strategy*. Rome, 10-12 May 2011

IFC (2006). *Small and Medium Enterprise Department, Background Note on Micro, Small and Medium enterprise database*, World Bank,

Washington

ILO (1998). Terms of employment and working conditions in health sector reforms.Geneva: ILO

—. (2012). *Start and Improve your Business: Global Tracer Study 2011: ILO's Business Management Training Programme.* Geneva: ILO

IMF, 2002: IMF Reviews Experience and Next Steps in the Fund's Transparency Policy. In: Public Information Notice 02/111.

—. (2010). *World Economic Outlook.* Washington, DC

—. (2011). *World Economic Outlook.* Washington, DC

Islamic Development Bank (1994), Promotion of Labour- Intensive Small-Scale Industries in Sierra Leone. Feasibility Study

Jaworski, J (1996). *Synchronicity: the Inner Path of Leadership* (San Francisco: Berrett Koehler, 1996)

Kallon, K.M.(1990),The Economies of the Sierra Leone Entrepreneurship. University Press of America, Lanhan, MD

Kanu, A.M. (2004), Coping With Rural Poverty: A Case Study of Sierra Leone. Unpublished Thesis, University of Gent, Belgium

Kaplan, R.S., and Norton, D.P. (1996). "Using the Balanced Scorecard as a Strategic Management System". *Harvard Business Review,* January-February 1996: 73-85.

Karlsson, C., Johannisson, B. and Storey, D. (1993), Small Business Dynamics: International, national and regional perspectives.Routledge, London

Kauffmann, C. (2005). Financing SMEs in Africa. Policy Insights, No. 7. OECD Development Center. Paris.

Kayanula, D. and Quartey, P. (2000). The Policy Environment for Promoting Small and Medium-Sized Enterprises in Ghana and Malawi, Paper No. 15, IDPM, University of Manchester

Kiggundu, M.N. (2002), Entrepreneurs and Entrepreneurship in Africa: What is Known and What Needs to be Done. Journal of Development entrepreneurship, Vol.7 No.3, P.239-258

Killick, T. (1998), Adjustment, income distribution and poverty in Africa: A research guide. Collaborative Research Project- Poverty, Income Distribution and Labour Market Issues in Sub-Saharan Africa

Klapper, F.D. (2002). *Small and Medium-Sized Enterprises Financing in Eastern Europe:* World Bank Policy Research Working Paper, 2933, December 2002

Knack, S, and Keefer, P. (1995). Institutions and Economic Performance: Cross-Country Tests Using Alternative Institutional Indicators. Economics and Politics , Vol. 7, No. 3 (November 1995): pp. 207-228.

Kwilecki, S. (1988). A scientific approach to religious development:

Proposals and a case illustration. *Journal for the Scientific Study of Religion, 27,* 307–325.

Liedholm, C, and Mead, D. (1987), Small-Scale Industries in Developing Countries: Empirical Evidence and Policy Implications. Michigan State University International Development Papers, Number 9

Lessem, R and Nussbaum, B (1996). *Sawubona Africa: Embracing Four Worlds in South African Management* (Johannesburg, South Africa; Zebra Press, Struik Publishers, 1996)

Lok-Dessallien, R. (1999), Review of Poverty Concepts and Indicators. UNDP. http://www.undp.org/poverty/publications/pov_red/Review_of _Poverty_Concepts.pdf

Luetkenhorst, W. (2004). Economic Development, the Role of SMEs and the Rationale for Donor Support: Some Reflection on Recent Trends and Best Practices. SME Partnership Group Meeting Hanoi, UNIDO.

Mass G, Herrington M (2006). *Global Entrepreneurship Monitor South African Executive Report* (online). Available: http://www.gbs.nct.ac.za/gbswebb/userfiles/gemsouthafrica2000pdf

Malhotra, K.(2004), Trade, Growth, Poverty Reduction and Human Development: Some Linkages and Policy Implications. UNDP, Palais des Nations, Geneva

Mamman, A; Baydoun, N and Asumah, B (2009). Transferability of management innovation to Africa: A study of two multinational companies' performance management system in Nigeria. *Global Business Review; 10 (1) pp. 1-31*

Manu, George (1998) Enterprise development in Africa - strategies for impact and growth, *Small Enterprise Development*, Volume 9, Number 4, December 1998, pp. 4-13(10)

Mbiti, J.S. (1991). *African Religions and Philosophy* (2nd Ed., New Hampshire, USA: Heinemann

McRobbie, G. (1981). *Small is Possible: St Edmundsbury Press.* Bury St Edmunds, Suffolk.

Mead, D.C.(1994), The Contribution of Small Enterprises to Employment Growth in Southern and Eastern Africa, Journal of World Development, Vol. 22, No.12, p.1881-1894

Mead, D.C. and Leidholm, C. (1998), The dynamics of Micro and Small Enterprises in Developing Countries. World Development, Vol 26, No.1 p 61-74

Miller-Stennett, Andrea M. (2003). *Informal Sector Training in Jamaica: An Assessment, In Focus Programme on Skills, Knowledge and Employability, Informal Economy Series*, International Labour Office, Geneva

Mintzberg, H. (1998). *Structure in Fives*. Prentice-Hall International.

Mitra, K (2003). Desirability of nominal GDP targeting under adaptive learning. *Journal of Money, Credit and Banking,* 35(2), 197-220

Mourkogiannis, N (2006). *Purpose: The Starting Point of Great Companies*. Palgrave/Macmillan, New York

Moyo, S. (2009). Dead Aid: Why Aid Is Not Working and How There Is a Better Way for Africa. Available at: http://www.carnegiecouncil.org/studio/multimedia/20090409/0142.ht ml/_res/id=sa_File1/

NTSIKA, (2002) State of Small Business Development in South Africa. *Annual Review 2002* Pretoria, NTSIKA Enterprise Promotion Agency

Nussbaum, B (2003). African Culture and *Ubuntu:* Reflections of a South African in America. Perspectives; vol. 17(1), pp. 1-12

ODI, (2010). Private sector for Development. *Overseas Development Institute Policy Brief*, May 2010

OECD, (2005). Promoting entrepreneurship and innovative smes in a global economy. Paris

—. (2006) *"Promoting Pro-poor Growth: Private Sector Development."* Paris

Oka, G. B. (1998).*Globalization from Hindu perspective*. In Camilleri, J.A. and Muzaffar, C. (eds.) Globalization: The perspectives and experiences of the religious Traditions of Asia pacific, Kuala Lumpur: International Movements for a Just World, p. 31-39.

Okpara, J.O. (2011). Factors Constraining the Growth and Survival of SMEs Nigeria: Implications for Poverty Alleviation. Management Research Reviews, 34(2), 156-171

Olawale, F. and Garwe, D. (2010) Obstacles to the Growth of New SMEs in South Africa: A principal component analysis approach. *African Journal of Business Management,* Vol. 4(5), pp. 729-738

Olson, E.M. & Slater, S.F. (2002). A fresh look at industry and market analysis: Understanding markets beyond the Five Competitive Forces Model. *Business Horizon*, 45(1), pp. 1-8

Olve, N.G; Petri, C.J., Roy, J. and Roy, S. (2004). Twelve Years Later: Understanding and Realizing the Value of Balanced Scorecards. *Ivey Business Journal;May/Jun2004,* Vol. 68 Issue 5, p1

Osei Boch–Ocansey, O (1996). *Strategies for strengthening small and medium-sized industries in Ghana*. Accra : Anansesem Publ. Ltd.

OXFAM. (2002*), Rigged Rules and Double Standards: Trade, Globalisation, and the Fight against Poverty*, London. Available at: http://www.maketradefair.com/assets/english/report_english.pdf.

Pargament, K.I and Park, C.L (1995). Merely a defense: variety of religious means and ends. *Journal of Social Issues, 51; 13-32*

Patterson, O (2006). Poverty of the Mind. *New York Times*. March, 26, 2006. Page 1-2

Piedmont, R. L. (1999). Does spirituality represent the sixth factor of personality? Spiritual transcendence and the five-factor model. *Journal of Personality*, 67, 985–1014.

Piron H and Evans, A (2005). Politics and the PRSP Approach: Synthesis Paper, Working Paper 237, London: Overseas Development Institute,.

Porter.M. E. (1980), Competitive Strategy: Techniques for Analysing Industries and Competitors. Macmillan, .New Work, London

—. (1985). *Competitive Advantage: Creating and sustaining superior performance*. Free Press. NY

Pradhan, N. C. (1989). Gender participation in irrigation system activities in the hills of Nepal. Proceedings of Second Annual Workshop on Women in Farming Systems, September 27-29,1989. Rampur, Chitwan, Nepal: Institute of Agriculture and Animal Science. Kathmandu, Nepal: United States Agency for International Development.

Randall, V. and Theobald, R. (1998). *Political change and underdevelopment: A critical introduction to Third World Politics*. London: Macmillan.

Ravnborg H. M. (2003). Poverty and Environmental Degradation in the Nicaraguan Hillsides. World Development Vol. 31, No. 11, p. 1933–1946

Ray, D. (1998), Development Economics. Princeton University Press, Princeton, USA

Riddell, R.C. (1987), Foreign Aid Reconsidered. The Johns Hopkins University Press

Robbins, S.P and Judge, T.A (2010). Organizational Behaviour. NJ: Prentice Hall

Rosenzwig, M.R. (1998). Labour Markets in Low-Income Countries. In Chenery, H.B. and Srinivasan, T.N. (eds), Handbook of Development Economics, Vol 1, Amsterdam, Holland

Rothwell, R. and Zegveld, W. (1982), Innovation and The Small and Medium-Sized Firm. Frances Pinter, London

Ruggles, P. (1990). Drawing the Line--Alternative Poverty Measures and Their Implications for Public Policy. Washington, D.C., Urban Institute Press

Sarwar, G.MD. (2002), Institutions and Poverty Reduction: A Case Study of Rural Bangladesh. PhD Thesis, Institute for Development Policy and Management, University of Manchester

Satha-Anand, C, (1998). *Spiritualising real Estate Commoditizing*

Pilgrimage: Globalization and Islamic Responses in Asia-Pacific? In Camilleri, J.A. and Muzaffar, C. (eds.) Globalization: The perspectives and experiences of the religious Traditions of Asia pacific, Kuala Lumpur: International Movements for a Just World, p.135-141.

Schay, B. W., Beach, M. E., Caldwell, J. A., & LaPolice, C. (2002). Using Standardized Outcome Measures in the Federal Government. *Revista: Human Resource Management* (New York), 41(3), 355-368.

Schelzig, K. (2005), Poverty in the Philippines: income, assets, and access. Asian Development Bank, Mandaluyong

Schmitz, H. (1995), Collective Efficiency: Growth Path for Small Scale Industry. *Journal of Development Studies*, Vol.31, no.4, p.529-566

Simon, M and King. K (1999) "Enterprise in Africa: new contexts; renewed challenges." *Enterprise in Africa-Between poverty and growth* 1.12 (1999):

SLEDIC, (2006). *Sierra Leone Export Development and Investment Corporation.* Freetown

Slife, B., Hope, C.,&Nebeker, S. (1997). *Examining the relationship between religious spirituality and psychological science.* Unpublished manuscript, Brigham Young University, Provo, UT.

Soledad and Peria (2009). Bank financing to SMEs: what are Africa's specificities?. *Propaco's Magazine*, Issue 1, May

Soros. G. (2002). On globalization. Public Affairs (Perseus Books Group). New York

South Africa Department of Trade and Industry. (1995), White Paper on National Strategy for the Development and Promotion of Small Business in South Africa, Pretoria

Steel, W.F. and Webster, L. (1990). Ghana's Small Enterprise Sector: Survey of Adjustment Response and Constraints. Industry Series Paper 14, World Bank, Industry and Energy Department, Washington D.C.

Stevenson L. and St-Onge, A. (2005). Support for Growth-Oriented Women Entrepreneurs in Kenya. International Labour Organisation

Stiglitz, J. (2006). *Making globalization work.* New York: W.W. Norton & Company.

Storey, D. (1994). *Human Resource Management: Critical text.* Oxford: Blackwell

Sunkel, O. (1972), The International Monetary System of the Year 2000. In: Bhagwati, J.N.(eds), *Economics and World Order-From the 1970's to the1990's*, Macmillan, New York, USA, p. 199-231

Sutton, J. (1997). Gibrat's Legacy. *Journal of Economic Literature*, Vol. 35, No.1, p. 40-59

The Economic Commission for Africa. (2005), Our Common Interest:

Report of the Commission of Africa

Thoburn, J. (2000). Finding the Right Track for Industry in Africa- Some Policy Issues and Options. Discussion Paper. UNIDO

Todaro, P.M and Smith, C.S. (2003). *Economic Development*, 8th Edition. Pearson Addison Wesley, U.K.

Tracy, B. (1993). *Maximum Achievement: Strategies and Skills that will unlock your hidden powers to succeed.* Simon & Schuster. NY.

—. (1996). Create your own future. N.J: John Wiley

—. (2003). *Change your Thinking, Change your Life: How to Unlock your Full Potential for Success and Achievement.* John Wiley & Sons. New Jersey.

—. (2010). *Goals: How to Get Everything You Want – Faster than You Ever Thought Possible.* Barrett-Koehler Publishers: San Francisco

UNIDO (2007). *Corruption prevention to foster small and medium-sized enterprise development – Providing anti-corruption assistance to small businesses in the developing world.* Vol.1.

—. (2010). Annual Report 2010.

—. (2011). The Youth to Youth Fund in West Africa. UNIDO, Vienna.

United Nations (2000). Millennium Development Goals. NY:

—. (2006), Small and Medium –Sized Enterprises in the Caucasian Countries in Transition: Experience in Armenia, Azerbaijan and Georgia. New York and Geneva. Available at: http://www.unece.org/indust/sme/caurep.pdf.

—. (2012). Millennium Development Goals. NY:

Van Dyk, A. C (2001). Traditional African beliefs and customs: implications for AIDS education and prevention in Africa. *South African Journal of Psychology.* Vol. 31(2), 60-66

Walsh, R and F. Vaughan. (1993) An introduction to common elements of transpersonal practices. *Journal of Transpersonal Psychology* 2:1-10,

Wickham, P.A (2004). *Strategic Entrepreneurship.* London: Pearson Education.

Whelan, B. J., and C.T. Whelan. (1995). In what sense is poverty multidimensional?. *Beyond the threshold.*

White, H and Killick, T. (2001), *African poverty at the millennium - causes, complexities and challenges.* Washington DC. World Bank

Woolard, I. (2002), An Overview of Poverty and Inequality in South Africa. *Working Paper prepared for* DFID (SA)

World Bank. (2001),*World Development Report* 2000/2001. Attacking Poverty, World Bank. Oxford University Press

—. (2003). Timor-Leste Assessment: Poverty in a New Nation – Analysis for, volume 1, *Main Report*, Washington DC

—. (2004), *Review of Small Business Activities*. Washington, D.C. World Bank

—. (2005). *Capacity Building in Africa: An OECD of World Bank Support*. Washington D.C.

—. (2006): *Making Finance work for Africa*, World Bank, Washington

—. (2009). *Global monitoring report: A development Emergency*. Washington D.C

—. (2013). *Worl Development Report: Jobs*. Washington D.C

World Development Report. (1990), Poverty. Oxford University Press, New York, World Bank

—. (2000/2001), World Bank: Causes of Poverty and a Framework for Action. Washington, D.C, USA

—. (2012). Gender Equality and Development. Washington, D.C, USA

—. (2013). end extreme poverty, promote shared prosperity. Washington, D.C, USA

Zagzebski, L.T (1996). *Virtues of the mind: an inquiry into the nature of virtue and ethical foundations of knowledge*. University of Cambridge